remembered

rapture

Also by bell hooks

Wounds of Passion: A Writing Life (1997)

Bone Black: Memories of Girlhood (1996)

Reel to Real: Race, Sex and Class at the Movies (1996)

Killing Rage: Ending Racism (1995)

Art of My Mind: Visual Politics (1995)

Outlaw Culture: Resisting Representation (1994)

Teaching to Transgress:
Education as the Practice of Freedom (1994)

Sisters of the Yam: Black Women and Self-Recovery (1993)

The Woman's Mourning Song (1993)

Black Looks: Race and Representation (1992)

Breaking Bread: Insurgent Black Intellectual Life (1991)

Yearning: Race, Gender, and Cultural Politics (1990)

Talking Back: Thinking Feminist, Thinking Black (1989)

Feminist Theory: From Margin to Center (1984)

Ain't I a Woman: Black Women and Feminism (1981)

remembered rapture

the writer at work

bell hooks

A Holt Paperback
Henry Holt and Company
New York

Holt Paperbacks
Henry Holt and Company, LLC
Publishers since 1866
175 Fifth Avenue
New York, New York 10010
www.henryholt.com

Earlier versions of some of the chapters in this book appeared in the following
publications: "Intellectual Life: In and Beyond the Academy," reprinted from
Z Magazine, November 1995; "A Life in the Spirit: Faith, Writing, and Intellectual
Work," reprinted from *Revision,* Winter 1993 (first published as "A Life in the Spirit").

Library of Congress Cataloging-in-Publication Data
Hooks, Bell.
Remembered rapture : the writer at work / Bell Hooks.
p.   cm.
ISBN-13: 978-0-8050-5910-6
ISBN-10: 0-8050-5910-5
1. Hooks, Bell.   2. American literature—Afro-American authors—History and
criticism.   3. American literature—Women authors—History and criticism.
4. United States—Intellectual life—20th century.   5. English teachers—United
States—Biography.   6. Afro-American women—Intellectual life.   7. Scholarly
publishing—United States.   8. Critics—United States—Biography.   9. Feminism—
United States.   10. Women—Authorship.   11. Authorship.   I. Title.
PE64.H66A3   1999   ·   98-7998
808'.02'082—dc21   CIP

Henry Holt books are available for special promotions and
premiums. For details contact: Director, Special Markets.

Originally published in hardcover in 1999 by
Henry Holt and Company

First Holt Paperbacks Edition 1999

Designed by Michelle McMillian

Printed in the United States of America

P1

words have weight—
you bear with me
the weight of my words
suffering whatever pain
this burden causes you
in silence—

i bow to you—

Rosa bell and Veodis Watkins

. . . when I ask you to write more books I am urging you to do what will be for your good and for the good of the world at large.

VIRGINIA WOOLF

contents

contents

preface

rapture from the deep

Writing these essays about writing has intensified my understanding and appreciation of the writer at work. This work was written to share the dimensions of my writing life that take place behind the scenes. Written from the standpoint of cultural critic, literary scholar, and/or creative writer, these essays probe and examine. They interrogate. Some are academic in tone, others are polemical or playful or just plain celebratory. They span a period of twenty years. Significantly, issues that were relevant and key when I first began writing are still central. Engaging these ideas through the years necessarily leads to some repetition. As a writer I come back to the same place again and again, hoping to make a new discovery or to see an old idea in a fresher light. When I am writing, when I am reading, I reflect on the process of writing itself. Like so much of my work, many of the essays in this collection emerged as responses to readers who wanted to know more about how the work came to be what it is and other less gentle interrogators who found my engagement with writing suspect.

Pondering why it is so many people find my (a black woman writer) passion for the written word suspect, I am reminded of how recent it is that we have made our literary voices heard in a sustained way—especially writing nonfiction. I write much about that in *Remembered Rapture*, dwelling on diverse subjects: the issue of labels, of whether one is a black or woman writer or just a writer; talking about why I write so much; discussing the social and political implications of writing by and about women emerging in the wake of contemporary feminist movement; probing the politics of confessional writing, the rise in popularity of the contemporary memoir. In several essays I look at the link between my writing and spiritual belief and practice. I write here about class and how our class background influences both what we write, how we write, and how the work is received. And finally I write about some of the women writers whose work and literary presence influences me, shaping the contours of my imagination, expanding the scope of my vision. No writer's work has touched my life as significantly as the work of Emily Dickinson, and it is time for me to give her praise. Two of the women writers I pay homage to, Toni Cade Bambara and Ann Petry, died in recent years; their passing was not recognized enough in the press as the tremendous loss to the world of American letters, for their work and presence illuminate very specific periods in our history as a nation—and the development of black women's writing.

In many of these essays I grapple with the issue of public work as an intellectual in and outside the academy and that space of writing that is always intimate, private, solitary. Again and again I return to the issue of voice—to break silence, to talk about the reality that black women's literary voices are here to stay even as we still confront a culture that is not yet fully ready to register and recognize the diversity and range of our vision. As a still emergent group of writers, especially in the area of nonfiction work, black women grapple continually with the suspicions of a larger literary world that is still not confident we are serious thinkers and writers. And then we confront one another, finding among ourselves that envy and fear often lead us away from the solidarity that is needed to ensure our work will not be once again relegated to an abyss of silence, dismissed once more as unnecessary, as irrelevant, as not good or good enough.

I address these issues in *Remembered Rapture* because the market-place has discovered our words are a useful commodity and eagerly seeks to push our work only in the direction of profit and gain. We have visions that must be protected and cherished, for we are still claiming our space in words—still seeking audiences that can take us and our work seriously, still waiting for a generation of publishers and critics to emerge who are not blinded by biases. Again and again in these essays I respond to the question most often asked me by everyone, Why do you write so much? I recall the words of Virginia Woolf, whose *A Room of One's Own* has always provided a guide and an anchor, urging us so long, so silent women to "write all kinds of books, hesitating at no subject however trivial or vast," telling us that if we "consider any great figure of the past, like Sappho, like the Lady Murasaki, like Emily Bronte" we will find "that she is an inheritor as well as an originator, and has come into existence because women have come to the habit of writing natu-rally. . . ." Ah! but my dear sister Virginia could never imagine black women writing "naturally." For like everyone she knew, our very existence on the landscape of Western literature was the outcome of unnatural acts.

No! Black women in the diaspora do not come to writing natu-rally, for there is always someone standing ready to silence the natu-ral impulse to create as it arises in us, and so to write we must ever resist. We must ever remember that our ancestors sacrificed that we might possess the skill to read—to write. No! Black women have not come to writing naturally for we have "come over a way that with tears has been watered, treading our feet through the blood of the slaughtered." We have come to writing through the suffering of our ancestors here on these shores. While this suffering does not sanctify us it does remind us that ours is a literary history where even the threat of death could not silence our passion for written words—our longing to read, to write, to know.

Writing about his life and the people who influenced him, black theologian and mystic Howard Thurman often focused on his maternal grandmother Nancy Ambrose, telling how she encouraged him to be a seeker after truth: ". . . I got from her an enormous respect for the magic that there is in knowledge. That came from what she had observed as a slave child. Whenever her owner's wife saw her daughter trying to teach my grandmother the alphabet or one, two, three, she would chastise the child and send her to bed without supper. My grandmother said: 'I saw there must be some magic in knowing how to read and write.'" Although she never learned to read or write she urged her grandson to acquire this magic and use it in the service of self-realization.

Like Howard Thurman, I was raised in a world where many of the teachers of wisdom around me were elder black women and men who could not read or write. As part of my religious missionary service it was often my designated task as a child to be the eyes for those who did not have eyes, the hands for those who could not write. No language adequately describes what it feels like to live in a world where so much depends on the written word and be unable to grasp the significance of those marks on paper. No words can convey the sense of powerlessness before the mystery of print. I witnessed the pain and shame of illiterate elders. Yet more than their anguish of spirit what I remember most is the intensity of their longing—their desire to be led into this world of written words. They never let me forget that they could not enter this world without a guide. And that my ability to guide them was a precious gift. They never let me forget that some of them had been to school but had not been "taught right" and so they did not come away from "learning" knowing how to make sense of words on the page. They never let me forget that I was blessed. To them words were sacred. To read and write was to partake of a sacrament as holy as our eating the body and drinking the blood of the divine in communion and remembrance.

That sense of the sacredness of words, of writing, has been inside my mind, heart, and imagination for such a long time. I can no longer remember a world without words on the page calling me, calling me to come inside and to find what Rilke named "the deeps into which your life takes rise." I knew then. I knew when I sat at the feet of Miss Zula, who could barely move because illness had caused her dark body had grown huge and monstrous, reading— letting my tongue and breath caress written words, giving voice to passions she would never know—I knew then I wanted a life in words. I wanted to be a writer. I wanted to be able to enter this sacred realm at will and find there the meaning of grace.

I did not wait for desegregation, for college, for creative-writing classes, for grown-ups to show me the way. I found my vocation. It called to me and I was determined to answer the call. I began to write in my girlhood. And I am writing still, moving swiftly into midlife with a body of words I have made into books beside me. No passion in my life has been as constant, as true as this love. No passion has been as demanding. When words call, to answer, to satisfy the urge, I must come again and again to a solitary place—a place where I am utterly alone. In that moment of grace when the words come, when I surrender to their ecstatic power, there is no witness.

Only I see, feel, and know how my mind and spirit are carried away. Only I know how the writing process alchemically alters me, leaving me transformed. Other writers tell of how it works within them. Written words change us all and make us more than we could ever be without them. Still the being we become in the midst of the very act of writing is only ever intimately present to the one who writes.

Writing about writing is one way to grasp, hold, and give added meaning to a process that remains one of life's great mysteries. I have not yet found words to truly convey the intensity of this remembered rapture—that moment of exquisite joy when necessary words come together and the work is complete, finished, ready to be read. I do know that I return again and again to that place, to that moment—to the rapture. That written words offer me this gift is an endless blessing.

remembered

rapture

writing from the darkness

I remember childhood as time in anguish, as a dark time—not darkness in any sense that is stark, bleak, or empty but as a rich space of knowledge, struggle, and awakening. We seemed bound to the earth then, as though like other living things our roots were so deep in the soil of our surroundings there was no way to trace beginnings. We lived in the county, in a space between city and country, a barely occupied space. Houses stood at a distance from one another, few of them beautiful; always a sense of isolation and unbearable loneliness hovered about them. We lived on hilly land, trees and wild honeysuckle hiding the flat spaces where gardens grew. I do not remember darkness there. It was the blackness enveloping earth and sky out in the country at Daddy Jerry's and Mama Willie's house that gave feeling and meaning to darkness. There it seemed textured, as though it were velvet cloth folded in many layers. That darkness had to be confronted as we made our way before bedtime to the outhouse. "No light necessary," granddaddy would say. "There is light in darkness, you just have to find it." That was early childhood. From then on I was terribly lost in an inner darkness as deep and thick as the blackness of those nights. I could not find my way or see the light there.

I was a child and his words had given me confidence. I believed with him that there was light in darkness waiting to be found. Later unable to find my way, I began to feel uncertain, displaced, estranged even. This was the condition of my spirit when I decided to be a writer, to seek for that light in words. No one understood. Coming from country black folks, seemingly always old, folks with the spirit of the backwoods, odd habits and odd ways, I had no way to share this longing—this ache to write words. In our world there was an intense passionate place for telling stories. It was really some big-time thing to be able to tell a good story, to as Cousin Bo would say "call out the hell in words." Writing had no such place. Writing the old people could not do even if they had been lucky enough to learn how. Folks wrote only when they had to; it was an awesome task, a burden. Making lists or writing letters could anguish the spirit. And who would anguish the spirit unnecessarily?

Searching for a space where writing could be understood, I asked for a diary. I remember early on getting the imitation-leather red or green books at holiday times, with DIARY written on them in bright gold letters, and of course there were those ever-so-tiny gold keys, two of them. Keys that were inevitably lost. Whole diaries gone because I refused to pry them open, not wanting what was private to be accessible. Confessional writing in diaries was acceptable in our family because it was writing that was never meant to be read by anyone. Keeping a daily diary did not mean that I was seriously called to write, that I would ever write for a reading public. This was "safe" writing. It would (or so my parents thought) naturally be forsaken as one grew into womanhood. I shared with them this assumption. Such writing was seen as a necessary stage but only

4

that. It was for me the space for critical reflection, where I struggled to understand myself and the world around me, that crazy world of family and community, that painful world. I could say there what was hurting me, how I felt about things, what I hoped for. I could be angry there with no threat of punishment. I could "talk back." Nothing had to be concealed. I could hold on to myself there.

However much the realm of diary-keeping has been a female experience that has often kept us closeted writers, away from the act of writing as authorship, it has most assuredly been a writing act that intimately connects the art of expressing one's feeling on the written page with the construction of self and identity, with the effort to be fully self-actualized. This precious powerful sense of writing as a healing place where our souls can speak and unfold has been crucial to women's development of a counter-hegemonic experience of creativity within patriarchal culture. Significantly, diary writing has not been traditionally seen by literary scholars as subversive autobiography, as a form of authorship that challenges conventional notions about the primacy of confessional writing as mere documentation (for women most often a record of our sorrows). Yet in the many cases where such writing has enhanced our struggle to be self-defining it emerges as a narrative of resistance, as writing that enables us to experience both self-discovery and self-recovery.

Faced with the radical possibility of self-transformation that confessional writing can evoke, many females cease to write. Certainly, when I was younger I did not respond to the realization that diary writing was a place where I could critically confront the "self" with affirmation. At times diary writing was threatening. For me the confessions written there were testimony, documenting realities I was not always able to face. My response to this sense of threat was to destroy the diaries. That destruction was linked to my fear that growing up was not supposed to be hard and difficult, a time of anguish and torment. Somehow the diaries were another accusing voice declaring that I was not "normal." I destroyed that writing and I wanted to destroy that tormented and struggling self. I did not understand, then, the critical difference between confession as an act of displacement and confession as the beginning stage in a process of self-transformation. Before this understanding, the diary as mirror was a place where that part of myself I could not accept or love could be named, touched, and then destroyed. Such writing was release. It took the terror and pain away—that was all. It was not then a place of reconciliation and reclamation.

None of the many diaries I wrote growing up exist today. They were all destroyed. Years ago when I began a therapeutic process of retrospective self-examination, I really missed this writing and mourned the loss. Since I use journals now as a way to engage in critical self-reflection, confrontation, and challenge, I know that I would be able to know myself differently were I able to read back, to remember with that writing. Those years of sustained diary writing were crucial to my later development as a writer for it was this realm of confessional writing that enabled me to find a voice. Still there was a frightening tension between the discovery of that voice and the assumption that, though expressed, it would then need to be concealed, contained, hidden, and ultimately destroyed. While I had been given permission to keep diaries, it was writing that my family began to see as dangerous when I began to express ideas considered strange and alien. Diaries provided a space for me to develop an autonomous voice and that meant such writing, once sanctioned, became suspect. It was impressed upon my consciousness that having a voice was dangerous. This was reinforced when my sisters would find and read my diaries, then deliver them to our mother as evidence that I was truly a mad person, an alien, a stranger in their household.

This tension between writing as an expression of my longing to emerge as autonomous creative thinker and the fear that such expression and any other manifestation of independence would mean madness, an end to life, created barriers between me and those written words. I was afraid of their power and yet I needed them. Writing was the only space where I could express myself freely. It was crucial to my fragile sense of well-being. I was often the family scapegoat—persecuted, ridiculed. I was often punished. It was as though I lived in a constant state of siege, subject to unprovoked and unexpected terrorist attacks. I lived in dread. Nothing I did was ever right. That constant experience of estrangement was deeply saddening. I was brokenhearted.

Writing was the healing place where I could collect the bits and pieces, where I could put them together again. It was the sanctuary, the safe place. Yet I could not make that writing part of an overall process of self-recovery. I was able to use it constructively only as an outlet for suppressed feeling. Knowledge that the writing could have enabled transformation was blocked by feelings of shame. I was ashamed that I needed this sanctuary in words. Confronting parts of my self there was humiliating. To me that confession was a process of unmasking, stripping the soul. It made me naked and vulnerable. Even though the experience was cleansing and redemptive, it was a process I could not fully affirm or celebrate. Feelings of shame compelled me to destroy what I had written. Diary writing, as a record of confession, brought me face to face with the shadow self, the one we spend lifetimes avoiding. I was ashamed that this "me" existed. I read my words. They were mirrors. I looked at the self represented there. Destroying the diaries, I destroyed that shadow. There was no trace of her, nothing that could bear witness. I could not embrace that inner darkness, find the light in it. I could not hold that being or love her.

Undoubtedly this process of destroying the diaries, and the self represented there, kept me from attempting suicide. There were times when I felt that death was the only way I could escape that inner darkness. I remember even now how much I longed to be rid of the wounded me, that secret shadow self. In Lyn Cowan's Jungian discussion of masochism she describes that moment when we learn to "embrace the shadow" as a necessary stage in the psychic journey leading to recovery and the restoration of well-being. She comments: "Jung said the shadow connects an individual to the collective unconscious, and beyond that to animal life at its most primitive level. The shadow is the tunnel, channel, or connector through which one reaches the deepest, most elemental layers of psyche." Confronting that shadow-self can both humiliate and humble. Humiliation in the face of aspects of the self we think are unsound, inappropriate, ugly, or downright nasty blocks one's ability to see the possibility for transformation that such a facing of one's reality promises.

That sense of profound shame evoked whenever I looked at the shadow-self portrayed in the writing was a barrier. It kept me stuck in the woundedness. Even though acknowledging that self in writing was a necessary anchor enabling me to keep a hold on life, it was not enough. That shame had to be let go before I could fully emerge as a writer because it was there whenever I tried to create, whether the work was confessional or not. When I left home to attend college I carried with me the longing to write. I knew then that I would need to work through these feelings of shame. One early journal entry from that time reads:

Writing, and the hope of writing pulls me back from the edges of despair. I believe insanity and despair are at times one and the same. And I hear the voices of my past telling me that I will go crazy, that I will end up in a mental institution—alone. I remember my oldest sister laughing, telling me that no one would visit me there, that "girl, you ought to stop." Stop thinking. Stop dreaming. Stop trying to experience and understand life. Stop living in the world of the mind. That day I had sat a hot iron on my arm. I was ironing our father's pajamas. They were collectively mocking me. I asked them to leave me alone. I pleaded with them, "Why can't I just be left alone to be me?" I did not want to be molded. I was something. And when the hot iron came down on my arm I did not feel it. I was momentarily carried away, pleading with them. I stood there in the hallway ironing and even when the stinging pain was there I continued to iron. I stood there struggling to hide the pain and sorrow, not wanting to cry, not wanting them to know how much it hurt. I was trying to be brave. I know now that an anguished heart is never a brave heart. It's like some wounded body part that keeps bleeding, that can't stop itself. Writing eases the anguish. It is my connection. Through it and with it I transcend despair.

Writing, whether confessional prose or poetry, was irrevocably linked in my mind with the effort to maintain well-being. I began writing poetry about the same time that I began keeping diaries. Poetry writing was radically different. Unlike confessional prose, one could use language in writing poetry to mask feelings, to hide the experiential reality leading one to create. Poems on the subject of death and dying did not necessarily make explicit to the reader that I was at times struggling with the issue of whether to stay alive. Poetry writing as creative process was intimately linked with the experience of transcendence. Unlike the diary writing, which became a space where I confronted pain, poetry was the way to move beyond it. I never destroyed poems because I felt there was nothing revealed there about the "me of me."

Then and now I remain a great admirer of Emily Dickinson, often marveling that she as living presence seemed always absent from her poems. To me they do not stand as a record of her experience but more as expressions of what I believe she felt was a fitting and worthy subject for poetry. Her poems are masks, together creating a collective drama where the self remains in the shadows, dark and undiscovered. It is difficult to look behind the poems, to see, to enter those shadows. Poetry writing may have been just that for Dickinson, the making of an enclosure—the poem as wall, a screen shielding her from the shadow-self. Perhaps there was for her no safe place, nowhere that the unnamed could be voiced, remembered, held. Even if it is there in the poems, we as readers cannot necessarily know or find it. What is clear is that writing was for Dickinson a way to keep a hold on life.

Writing that keeps us away from death, from despair, does not necessarily help us to be well. Anne Sexton could confess, "I am trying a flat mask to hold my sanity up . . . my life is falling through a sieve" and then "the thing that seems to be saving me is the poetry." I remember her, Sylvia Plath, and not so well-known black women poets Georgia Douglas Johnson and Clarissa Scott Delany because they all struggled with dangerous melancholy and killing despair. We know that poetry does not save us, that writing does not always keep us away from death, that the sorrow of wounds that have never healed, excruciating self-doubt, or overwhelming melancholy often crushes the spirit, making it impossible to stay alive. Julia Kristeva speaks about women's struggle to find and sustain creative voice in the chapter "I Who Want Not to Be," which is part of the introduction to *About Chinese Women*. There she addresses the tension between our longing to "speak as women," to have being that is strong enough to bear the identity *writer*, and the coercive imposition of a feminine identity within patriarchy that opposes such being. Within patriarchy woman has no legitimate voice. Her voice is either constructed in complicity or resistance. If the choice is not radical then we speak only what the patriarchal culture would have us say. If we do not speak as liberators we collapse under the weight of this effort to speak within patriarchal confines or lose ourselves without dying. Kristeva recalls the Russian poet Marina Tsvetayeva, who hanged herself, writing: "I don't want to die. I want not to be." Her words echo my longing to be rid of the shadow-self, the "me of me."

Writing enables us to be more fully alive only if it is not a terrain wherein we leave the self—the shadows behind, escaping. Anne Sexton reiterated again and again in her letters that it was crucial that the writer keep a hold on life by learning to face reality: "I think that writers must try not to avoid knowing what is happening. Everyone has somewhere the ability to mask the events of pain and sorrow. . . . But the creative person must not use this mechanism any more than they have to in order to keep breathing." A distinction must be made between that writing which enables us to hold on to life even as we are clinging to old hurts and wounds and that writing which offers to us a space where we are able to confront reality in such a way that we live more fully. Such writing is not an anchor that we mistakenly cling to so as not to drown. It is writing that truly rescues, that enables us to reach the shore, to recover.

To become a writer I needed to confront that shadow-self, to learn ways to accept and care for that aspect of me as part of a process of healing and recovery. I longed to create a groundwork of being that could affirm my struggle to be a whole self and my effort to write. To fulfill this longing I had to search for that shadow-self and reclaim it. That search was part of a process of long inward journeying. Much of it took place in writing. I spent more than ten years writing journals, unearthing and restoring memories of that shadow-self, connecting the past with present being. This writing enabled me to look myself over in a new way, without the shame I had experienced earlier. It was no longer an act of displacement. I was not trying to be rid of the shadows, I wanted instead to enter them. That encounter enabled me to learn the self anew in ways that allowed transformation in consciousness and being. Resurrecting the shadow-self, I could finally embrace it, and by so doing come back to myself.

That woundedness that I was once so ashamed to recognize became for me a place of recovery, the dark deeps into which I could enter to find both the source of that pain and the means to heal. Only in fully knowing the wound could I discover ways to attend to it. Writing was a way of knowing. After what seemed like endless years of journal writing about the past, I wrote a memoir of my girlhood. It was indeed the culmination of this effort to accept the past and yet surrender its hold on me. This writing was redemptive. I no longer need to make this journey again and again.

women who write
too much

There are writers who write for fame. And there are writers who write because we need to make sense of the world we live in; writing is a way to clarify, to interpret, to reinvent. We may want our work to be recognized, but that is not the reason we write. We do not write because we must; we always have choice. We write because language is the way we keep a hold on life. With words we experience our deepest understandings of what it means to be intimate. We communicate to connect, to know community. Even though writing is a solitary act, when I sit with words that I trust will be read by someone, I know that I can never be truly alone. There is always someone who waits for words, eager to embrace them and hold them close.

For the vast majority of my life I have longed to write. In my girlhood writing was the place where I could express ideas, opinions, beliefs that could not be spoken. Writing has then always been where I have turned to work through difficulties. In some ways writing has always functioned in a therapeutic manner for me. In

The Dancing Mind, Toni Morrison suggests that the therapeutic ways writing can function are at odds with, or at least inferior to, a commitment to writing that is purely about the desire to engage language imaginatively. She contends: "I have always doubted and disliked the therapeutic claims made on behalf of writing and writers. . . . I know now, more than I ever did (and I always on some level knew it), that I need that intimate, sustained surrender to the company of my own mind while it touches another. . . ." Morrison's description of the urge that leads to writing resonates with me. Still, I believe that one can have a complete imaginative engagement with writing as craft and still experience it in a manner that is therapeutic; one urge does not diminish the other. However, writing is not therapy. Unlike therapy, where anything may be spoken in any manner, the very notion of craft suggests that the writer must necessarily edit, shape, and play with words in a manner that is always subordinated to desired intent and effect. I call attention to the way writing has functioned therapeutically for me as a location where I may articulate that which may be difficult, if not impossible to speak in other locations because this need leads me to turn and turn again to the written words and partially explains the sheer volume of my written work.

As long as I had only written and published one or two books no one ever inquired or commented on my writing process, on how long it took me to complete the writing of a book. Once I began to write books regularly, sometimes publishing two at the same time, more and more comments were made to me about how much I was writing. Many of these comments conveyed the sense that I was either doing something wrong by writing so much, or at least engaged in writing acts that needed to be viewed with suspicion. When I first took creative-writing classes from women professors who taught from a feminist perspective, we were encouraged to examine the way that sexism had always interfered with women's creativity, staging disruptions that not only limited the breadth and range of women's writing but the quantity as well. In a feminist studies course taught by writer Tillie Olsen I learned reading her essays on writing that prior to the 1960s it was rare if a white female writer, or a black female or male writer, published more than one book. We talked in class both about the material conditions that "silence" writers as well as the psychological barriers (i.e., believing that work will not be received or that what one has to say is either not important or has already been said). Knowing that black writers had faced difficulties that inhibited their capacity to write or complete works that had been started did serve as a catalyst challenging me to write against barriers—to complete work, to not be afraid of the writing process.

To overcome fears about writing, I began to write every day. My process was not to write a lot but to work in small increments, writing and rewriting. Of course I found early on that if I did this diligently these small increments would ultimately become a book. In *The Writing Life*, Annie Dillard reminds readers: "It takes years to write a book—between two and ten years. Less is so rare as to be statistically insignificant. One American writer has written a dozen major books over six decades. . . . Out of a human population on earth of four and a half billion perhaps twenty people can write a book in a year." Dillard's numbers may no longer be accurate as writers today not only have more time to write but have more writing aids (like the computer). Certainly as a writer who has handwritten, then typed or keyed into computer, all my books, I know how the computer and printer speed up the process. Typing and retyping a book takes much more time than keying in rewrites on a computer. I never approach writing thinking about quantity. I think about what it is I want to say. These days when I see the small yet ample stack of books I have written (usually seen at book signings), I know that this body of work emerged because I am again and again overwhelmed by ideas I want to put in writing. Since my interests are broad and wide-ranging, I am not surprised that there is an endless flow of ideas in my mind.

I write as one committed simultaneously to intellectual life, which means that ideas are the tools I search out and work with to create different and alternative epistemologies (ways of knowing). That I am continuously moved to share these ideas, to share thought processes in writing is sometimes as much a mystery to me as it is to readers. For I have writing comrades who work with ideas in the mind as much as I do but who are not as driven as I am to articulate those ideas in writing. A driving force behind my writing passion is political activism. Contrary to popular assumption writing can function as a form of political resistance without in any way being propagandistic or lacking literary merit. Concurrently, writing may galvanize readers to be more politically aware without that being the writer's sole intent.

A covert form of censorship is always at work when writing that is overtly espousing political beliefs and assumptions is deemed less serious or artistically lacking compared to work that does not overtly address political concerns. In our culture practically every aspiring writer realizes that work that is not addressing the status quo, the mainstream, that addresses unpopular political standpoints will rarely be given attention. It certainly will not make the best-seller list. Since I began my writing career utterly uninterested in writing anything other than poetry and fiction, work that I did not see as political, I was more acutely aware than most writers

16

might be that by writing critical essays on unpopular political issues, I might never be seen by the mainstream world of critics and readers as an artistically "serious" writer. It has been challenging to maintain a commitment to dissident writing while also writing work that is not overtly political, that aspires to be more purely imaginative.

Successful writing in one genre often means that any work done in another genre is already marked as less valuable. While I have been castigated for writing critical essays that are too radical or simplistic, just "wrong-minded," the poetry I write along with other work that does not overtly address political concerns is often either ignored or castigated for not being political enough. Until we no longer invest in the conventional assumption that a dichotomy exists between imaginative writing and nonfiction work, writers will always feel torn. Writers will always censor their work to push it in the direction that will ensure it will receive acclaim. Everyone knows that dissident writing is less likely to bring literary recognition and reward.

Dissident voices are rarely published by mainstream presses. Many writers from marginal groups and/or with unpopular perspectives have relied on small presses to publish their work. Indeed, my writing would not have achieved public acclaim were it not for the alternative small presses publishing my work at a time when large publishing houses simply held to the conviction that writing about race and gender would not sell. Mainstream publishers showed interest in my writing only after sales of work published with small presses documented that an established book-buying audience existed. Significantly, the publication of my work by a mainstream press was also possible because many young college-educated workers in the industry were familiar with the work

17

because they had studied it in school or knew that other students were excited about it and they could affirm the existence of an established readership.

My zeal for writing has intensified over the years and the incredible affirming feedback from readers is one catalyst. In my early writing years I thought this zeal was purely a function of will. However I found that rejection by the publishing world really affected my capacity to write. It left me feeling blocked, as though no one wanted to hear my ideas. No writer writes often or well if they despair of ever having an audience for their work. Knowing that readers want to hear my ideas stimulates my writing. While it does not lead me to write if I am uninspired, it does enhance my capacity to work when inspired. Long solitary hours spent writing feel more worthwhile when a writer knows there are eager readers waiting for new work. Oftentimes I write about issues readers have repeatedly asked me questions about at public lectures. My professorial work, which includes both classroom settings and public lectures, keeps me in closer touch with reader response to my work than I might be were I creating work in a more isolated manner. It is equally true that engaged dialogue about ideas is also a stimulant for writing. Sometimes I feel an urgent need to write ideas down on paper to make room for new ideas to arrive, keep my mind from becoming too crowded.

Historically the writers in our culture who were the most prolific were white males. Now this is changing. However, as more writers from marginal groups break silences or barriers that led to the creation of only one work, producing a body of work is often viewed with disdain or disparagement. While it is true that market forces lead the publishing industry to encourage writers to produce books that may simply be repetitive, poorly written, and uninspired simply because anything specific successful writers write will sell, it does not follow from this that every writer who has an ample body of work is merely responding to market-driven demands. Since I have never tried to make a living as a writer, I have had the extreme good fortune to be able to write only what I want to write when I want to write it. Not being at the mercy of the publishing industry to pay the rent or put food on the table has meant that I have had enormous freedom to resist attempts by the industry to "package" my work in ways that would be at odds with my artistic vision. Reflecting on the interplay between writing and the marketplace in *Art {Objects}*, Jeanette Winterson comments: "Integrity is the true writer's determination not to buckle under market forces, not to strangle her own voice for the sake of a public who prefers its words in whispers. The pressures on young writers to produce to order and to produce more of the same, if they have had a success, is now at overload, and the media act viciously in either ignoring or pillorying any voice that is not their kind of journalese." When I choose to write an essay book that includes work that may have been published first in magazines, reviewers will often write about the work as though it is stale, nothing new. A book of mine might include ten new essays (which alone could be a book) and four or five pieces that were published elsewhere and a reviewer might insist that there is no new work in the collection. Men can produce collections in which every piece has been published elsewhere and this will not even be mentioned in reviews. This critical generosity cuts across race. Two books that come to mind are Cornel West's collection *Race Matters* and Henry Louis Gates Jr.'s book *Thirteen Ways of Looking at a Black Man*. While feminist intervention altered the nature of contemporary women's writing, it has had little impact on critical evaluations of that work in the mainstream press.

Dissident writing is always more likely to be trashed in mainstream reviews. Rarely do mainstream critiques of my work talk about the content of the writing—the ideas. It took years of writing books that were published by alternative presses for this work to be acknowledged by the mainstream publishing world. Had I stopped writing early on it is unlikely that my books would ever have received any notice in mainstream culture. Ironically, producing a body of work has been one of the reasons it has not been easy for critics to overlook my writing even as they often imply in written critique and conversation that I should write less. Usually these critics are other women. While contemporary feminism highlighted difficulties women writers face by challenging and intervening on institutionalized barriers, it also opened up new possibilities (i.e., women's presses, more women entering the field of publishing). The incredible success of feminist and/or women's writing in the marketplace certainly compelled mainstream publishers to reconsider old approaches to writing by and about women. It is simply easier for women writers to write and sell work than ever before. As a consequence it has become more difficult for women to attribute failure to write or sustain creativity solely to sexist biases. These changes have led to conflict and competition between women who write a lot and those who do not, especially when the latter attribute nonproduction to sexist barriers. The harshest critics of my work have been less well-known black women writers and/or individuals who have had difficulty producing new work.

Like other women writers, who face barriers but surmount them to do the work they feel called to do, I find it disheartening when our literary triumphs however grand or small are not seen as part of a significant advance for all women writers. Until the prolific female writer, and more specifically the black female writer, is no longer seen as an anomaly we cannot rest assured that the degree of gender equity that exists currently in the writing and publishing world is here to stay. And while women writers should not be in any way fixated on the notion of quantity, we all should feel utterly free to write as much as time, grace, and the imagination allow.

Time remains a central concern for all women writers. It is not simply a question of finding time to write—one also writes against time, knowing that life is short. Like the poet Donald Hall I was enchanted by the Scripture that admonishes us to "work while it is day for the night cometh when no man can work." Even as a child these words made an impression. They haunted my own search for discipline as a writer. In his memoir *Life Work* Hall contemplates the relation between writing and dying, stating that "if work is no antidote to death, nor a denial of it, death is a powerful stimulus to work. Get done what you can." Annie Dillard urges us to "write as if you were dying." A large number of black women writers both past and present have gone to early graves. To know their life stories is to be made aware of how death hovers. When I was a young girl I studied the lives of writers I admired hoping to find guidance for my work. One of my favorite literary mentors was the playwright and critical thinker Lorraine Hansberry, who died in her mid-thirties. Her essay "The Negro Writer and His Roots" posed challenging questions for a young writer and intellectual. Hansberry declared: "The foremost enemy of the Negro intelligentsia of the past has been and remains—isolation. No more than can the Negro people afford to imagine themselves removed from the most pressing world issues of our time—war and peace, colonialism, capitalism vs. socialism—can I believe that the Negro writer imagines that he will be exempt from artistic examination of questions which plague the intellect and spirit of man." Of course, I often pondered the paths Hansberry might have taken had she lived longer. Her death and the early deaths of Pat Parker, Audre Lorde, Toni Cade Bambara, to name only a few, stand as constant reminders that life is not promised—that it is crucial for a writer to respect time.

Without urgency or panic, a writer can use this recognition to both make the necessary time for writing and make much of that time.

Like many writers, I am protective of the time I spend writing. Even though women write more today than ever before, most women writers still grapple with the issue of time. Often writing is the task saved for the end of the day. Not just because it is hard to value writing time, to place it above other demands, but because writing is hard. Oftentimes the writer seeks to avoid the difficulties that must be faced when we work with words. Although I have written many books, writing is still not easy. Writing so much has changed me. I no longer stand in awe of the difficulties faced when working with words, overwhelmed by the feeling of being lost in a strange place unable to find my way or crushed into silence. Now I accept that facing the difficult is part of the heroic journey of writing, a preparation, a ritual of sanctification—that it is through this arduous process of grappling with words that writing becomes my true home, a place of solace and comfort.

a body of work

women labor with words

Charis, my favorite women's bookstore, is in Atlanta, Georgia. It's collectively owned and operated. The moment I walk through the doors I feel it's a place where I belong, a place where I will always be welcomed. I have been buying books there for a long time. Yet I am still awed by the fact that an incredible number of the books on the shelves there by and about women were written in the last twenty years. At the very beginning of contemporary feminist movement a major focus of our critical energy was the recovery of "her-story." The movement was uncovering layers of writing by women that patriarchal biases in the literary world had long ago buried and forgotten. Revolutionary feminist movement changed all that. It dared to resurrect women's words. Not only did it encourage the recovery of literature by women that was lost, it encouraged women to write both about the past and present. Work by black woman writer Zora Neale Hurston had long been forgotten before feminist thinkers and publishers called attention to it. Singlehandedly, Alice Walker launched a campaign to restore

Hurston to her rightful place in American literature. When this renaissance initially occurred it was incredible. It was as though a hunt for buried treasure was taking place. Beautiful and precious gems were there to be discovered.

I remember sitting at reading groups with other women involved in women's liberation where some of us wept that books like Hurston's *Their Eyes Were Watching God* and Kate Chopin's *The Awakening* had been lost because they had not been valued by the male-dominated literary establishment. We wept not only because we had been deprived but also at the miracle of finding these literary treasures in our lifetime. It is awesome to think about the continued gap that would have been sustained in our literary canons if feminist movement had not created a revolution challenging the ways we think about knowledge and women's place in history.

Feminist movement to recover women's lost history has been one of the most triumphant aspects of contemporary women's rights struggle. Even though this profound cultural transformation occurred only twenty years ago, a large body of women's writing was so quickly unearthed and so much new writing emerged that the reading public has almost forgotten what a new phenomenon the valuation of women's words and our writing really is. Much of the awe I feel when walking through women's bookstores across the nation stems from the reality that so many of the books that I see have been written in the last twenty years. Most of these books focus on the experiences of white women in the United States. Even though black women and women of color are publishing more than ever before there is still a dearth of material from our perspectives. Despite all the recent contributions there is still not enough writing by and about black women. More work needs to be uncovered. There are so many lives that need to be written about and many new voices that need to be heard. Whenever I meet black females who have compelling visions, who have knowledge of our collective buried to share or moving personal stories, I urge them to write. I plead with them to put it down somewhere in journal and diaries, just put it somewhere. Not all writing has to be done with immediate publication in mind. We write to leave legacies for the future.

Zora Neale Hurston has become one of the most canonized black women writers in American literature today. Even though she died only a short while ago there is still so much about her personal history that we do not know and will never know. To this day much of who she was and how she lived is still shrouded in mystery. Even though scholars continue searching for material it will take years of research to uncover details about periods in her life that are still a mystery. Despite canonization Hurston's work still has not received the full range of scholarly attention it deserves. There should be a number of biographies about her work appearing, as well as a body of feminist critical readings of her material, yet there are only a few such books.

One can only speculate about the reasons for this. If indeed the primary audience interested in recuperating lost material about her life and work continues to be primarily progressive scholars, most of whom are women, there are few rewards and incentives for such work. Now that individual thinkers can no longer receive kudos for "rediscovering" Hurston, interest has waned. And of course there are never readily available resources to conduct such work. Concurrently, the scholars who have the best access to these resources are interested in other writers. Hurston's first biographer was white and male. When his book was published, he openly admitted that he felt there were blind spots in his perspective and stated that he looked forward to the progressive interpretive visions women scholars, particularly black women, could bring to Hurston's life and work. Such work has yet to appear. As institutions, professors, and students lean in conservative directions, choosing to focus on any woman writer of color is more risky. When this is coupled with the decreasing numbers of black scholars, it is even more doubtful that Hurston will ever receive the wealth of attention necessary for her work to be fully explored and understood. Yet it should never be forgotten that were it not for the passion and power of feminist movement, of women readers as book buyers, Hurston's work might have simply remained a buried treasure.

Long before mainstream bookstores focused on the growing body of published writing by and about women, the feminist bookstore celebrated and acknowledged this work. Significantly the continued existence of women's bookstores guards against a return to the days when patriarchal biases in publishing and marketing meant that one had to search hard and long for books by women authors. Another special aspect of the women's bookstore is the visual impact felt by all of us who enter and see shelves and shelves of women's writing. It is simply inspiring. However, the recognition that the majority of the books are by and about white women reminds us also that there is still a dearth of writing by and about black women/women of color.

Unfortunately the phenomenal successes of individual black women, writers like Toni Morrison, Alice Walker, Terry McMillan, and Maya Angelou, lead the reading public to assume that there is a wellspring of published writing by and about black women. In actuality, pulp fiction, self-help, and tabloid-like personal stories written by black women are on the increase. However, there is little significant increase in the publication of serious writing, both fiction and nonfiction, by black female authors. Publishing fifteen nonfiction books that were well received and well read was one of the triumphant moments of my writing career. Nonfiction writing is not regarded by the publishing industry as the strong suit of black women writers. Globally, the most well-known black women writers from this country are novelists. Even though they may write nonfiction, this writing did not gain them national attention. In actuality, throughout the diaspora black female authors mainly receive attention for works of fiction.

With no acknowledged established intellectual traditions, save contemporary ones, and even those are not widely acknowledged, black women writers of nonfiction working within the cultural context of white supremacist capitalist patriarchy have historically needed the interest of white readership to gain a hearing. It is no accident of history that I first established my presence as a writer of nonfiction with feminist work. White women, as a majority book-buying public, were the primary market for that work early on. Just as the rediscovery of Hurston's writing depended on engagement by white female readers who constituted an already established book-buying market, initially contemporary black women writers doing serious work, whether fiction or non fiction, benefited from feminist demands that women listen to one another's voices across the boundaries of race and class.

A willingness on the part of a mass audience in this society to take nonfiction writing by black women seriously came in the wake of the success of serious fiction writers, particularly the work of Toni Morrison. In general, the biases of racism and sexism as well as class elitism led the American public to feel that black women's voices are the least compelling when serious issues are at stake. While the unprecedented success of Michele Wallace's first book, *Black Macho and the Myth of the Superwoman,* in the late seventies appeared to usher in a new day for the black writer of nonfiction, the reading public seemed to be mainly interested in her take on black masculinity. Even though she continued to do insightful nonfiction writing about diverse subjects, the work did not capture the attention of a large public. Importantly, Wallace offered a necessary intellectual critique of black female "invisibility" wherein she calls attention to our struggle to come to voice in a society that is not yet prepared to fully receive our words and understand the way in which that poor reception acts to silence and repress.

Despite the clarity of her insight about the workings of race, sex, and class as structures of domination, Wallace has often directed her rage about silencing and denied access at other black women writers as though we control public reception of our work. Much of her work has been about naming this absence of control. Aggressively interviewed in the magazine *Konch* by a black male writer whose intent was to challenge the notion that black female writing does not gain a fair hearing, Wallace elucidates the various reasons our voices are often not heard or welcomed. She contends: "It's not only that the mainstream, the dominant society denies us access, we deny ourselves. We deny ourselves because we also feel that certain things should not be spoken in public." Sadly, Wallace suggests that one of the primary forces of repression that makes it difficult for black women writers to produce work has been unduly harsh responses in the press, citing the impact of reviews of her first book as a prime example. Yet she has written some of the most vicious comments and out-and-out trashings of her writing peers. Nothing diminishes our efforts to gain a greater hearing for nonfiction by black women more than the severe dismissals of this work by black women. It is no accident that periodicals that rarely review such work choose when they do to seek out individuals known to harbor competitive feelings or antipathy towards a writer, as that makes for colorful copy without really challenging the status quo.

The white editors who choose individual reviewers and set the guidelines tend to deploy this strategy to ensure against charges of racist and sexist biases.

Throughout my writing career some of the most spiteful and careless reviews of my work have been written by fellow black women writers. I want to make a clear distinction here between the huge audience of black women readers who support my work and that tiny minority writing reviews. It is often in the interest of a racially biased marketplace and media to pit us against one another. Black women writers of nonfiction who accept the notion, informed by racist/sexist biases, that there is only one slot, only one of us who can receive meaningful attention at a given moment in time, are primed to make their peers targets. Progressive black women writers resist this manipulation. This means that the will to subject black women's writing to forms of aggressive policing has to be continually interrogated. While we may disagree and critique one another, respect for the significance of an individual's writing coupled with awareness of the cultural context enables us to be critically vigilant.

Among my critics, individual black women tend to be the most vociferous in their insistence that I write "too much." Glibly, Jewelle Gomez began a critique of my thirteenth book by facetiously labeling me "the Joyce Carol Oates of black feminist writing." Wrongly, she suggested that the book was merely a recyling of already published work. In actuality, it was a collection of twenty-two essays in which six were reprinted. Had they not been included it would still have been a book-length manuscript. A little investigation on her part would have uncovered accurate information. However, possessing the correct information would have militated against glib dismissal. Often the suggestion that I am writing "too much" comes from black women who have either written very little or not as much as they want to write. Fortunately I have never had to write to make a living. As a consequence I have always only written on subjects that intrigue and fascinate me. From girlhood on I have felt that there were many subjects I wanted to write about. Passion for those subjects has inspired sustained writing. Like most writers, I would rather write and publish one well-written book than many poorly written ones. While quantity should never be seen as more important than quality, it is equally true that when the issue is nonfiction by women, particularly black women, there is an abundance of work that needs to be written. Significantly, no black woman writer, or anyone else for that matter, critiqued me for writing too much during the many years when I published books that sold well but did not bring national recognition. The continued success of the writing, the accolades it brings as well as the financial rewards seem to be most disturbing to the critical observers. When work is well conceived and well written it should not matter how many books the author has written.

No black woman writer in this culture can write "too much." Indeed, no woman writer can write "too much." Considering the centuries of silence, the genres of writing that have been virtually the sole terrain of men, more contributions by women writers should be both encouraged and welcomed. As a professor I sit in classrooms year after year talking with young women who are uncertain about their voices, who are still grappling with whether they can become "authors." Many of these young women are afraid to speak, let alone write. When I witness their fear, their silences, I know no woman has written enough. Then there are the exceptional female students who are unable to complete their own writing, who are blocked when it comes to putting their visions on paper, who diligently write work for their male peers or older men who require assistance, yet these females remain too shy to claim their words.

When I witness this self-betrayal, I know no woman has written enough.

Feminist activists struggled long and hard to create a space in contemporary culture where a woman writer's words can matter as much as those of any man. This struggle continues. Even though more women write and publish these days there are still styles and genres of writing we are not yet comfortable with. More recently, women who write against the grain, who challenge conventional assumptions about the female mind are often harshly critiqued by women readers who are discomfited by these new narratives. That discomfort has been registered recently as women critics respond to new novels by women authors where sexual scenes or violent acts are graphically described. Public reception of A. M. Homes's novel *The End of Alice* is one example. Works by women writers that challenge conventional sexist understandings of the female imagination tend to disturb readers the most. More frequently than not these works are interrogated by critical readers in ways that actively promote censure and silencing. The tone of reviews suggest these women have stepped out of place.

Unfortunately, more and more women seem all too eager to police female desire for words. I receive the message that it's fine to write but to be too devoted to writing makes me suspect. After my tenth book I began to notice how often individuals would come up to me and make snide comments about my writing "yet another book." They never hear me no matter how many times I share with them that writing is my passion. Like all passions it demands discipline and devotion. When I publish collections of essays where pieces are included that have been published elsewhere, reviewers will sometimes suggest that there is nothing new in these works. Yet collections by women who write much less, whose articles may have all been published elsewhere do not get dismissed as mere recycling. And men, no one mentions the absence of "fresh" work in their collections. Women who write a lot and women who write in a manner that transgresses traditional boundaries pose a threat precisely because our work stands as a serious challenge to sexist stereotypes.

While the capitalist marketplace acknowledges the power of women as consumers (white women are primary book buyers), overall the publishing industry continues to uphold patriarchal hegemony. Most books that receive high-paying advances and central attention in mass media are by white male authors. While privileged white women have made great strides, considering their primacy as consumers of books and as workers in the publishing industry more meaningful transformations should be taking place. Instead, without changing the basic belief structures (and that includes the biases of patriarchal thinking) the mainstream publishing industry simply appropriated the awareness of a market for books by and about women that feminist movement generated. Feminists encouraged women to write—to produce the desired commodity. Significantly, it was only after alternative publishing venues, particularly feminist presses, showed that big bucks could be made from the sale of such literature that this appropriation by mainstream publishing took place.

Undoubtedly, as long as market forces recognize that writing by women sells, there will be a plethora of published books. Yet this does not mean that the bulk of that writing will be serious work or that any of it will be writing from a feminist perspective. The more successful antifeminist backlash is, the harder it will be for work that is overtly feminist to gain a hearing. Women readers and our allies in struggle need to remember that writing by and about women is not the same as progressive and/or feminist writing by and about women from a feminist perspective. Indeed, while we have seen an incredible increase in the publication of books by women there is a decline in the number of nonacademic books that are written from a feminist perspective. Even in academic circles it has become much more fashionable to do work on gender rather than work that is distinctly feminist in outlook. Readers need to be mindful of this trend. If the crisis in publishing continues and the need to publish fewer books increases, dissident writing of any sort will find it hard to gain a hearing—that includes work inspired by feminist thinking. Mainstream publishing's takeover of alternative and/or subversive literatures threatens to silence alternative spaces. Now that masses of readers can buy books by feminist authors at mainstream bookstores many alternative spaces like women's bookstores have been forced to close. Yet if the audience for such work declines it is likely that mainstream sellers will refuse to house this material as they once did. For this reason supporting alternative publishers and bookstores remains an important gesture of progressive political activism. Most importantly we must not let the commercial success of writing by women lead us to believe that the struggle to create and maintain a culture where women's words will be heard and valued is over. That struggle continues. Hence the importance of women writing whenever we can, saying whatever we have to say, writing as much as we need to write.

If we were not in the midst of mounting antifeminist backlash, all the talk of women writing "too much" or in unacceptable ways could just be ignored. Instead, women writers and all our readers must talk back to all attempts to mock and belittle our commitment to words, to writing. These gestures are strategies of silencing; they devalue and undermine. In these times there should be no need for any female to fear putting words on paper. Although there are many critics who like to proclaim that there is an excess of writing by women—too much confession, too many women telling our stories—the truth remains that there is still much that has not been written by women, and about women's perspectives and experiences both past and present. There is a world of thoughts and ideas women have yet to write about in nonfiction—whole worlds of writing we need to enter and call home. No woman is writing too much. Women need to write more. We need to know what it feels like to be submerged in language, carried away by the passion of writing words.

remembered rapture

dancing with words

Writing is my passion. It is a way to experience the ecstatic. The root understanding of the word *ecstasy*—"to stand outside"—comes to me in those moments when I am immersed so deeply in the act of thinking and writing that everything else, even flesh, falls away. The metaphysics of writing has always enchanted me. Experiencing language as a transformative force was not an awareness that I arrived at through writing. I discovered it through performance—dramatically reciting poems or scenes from plays. At our all-black southern segregated schools the art of oration was deemed important. We were taught to perform. At school and at home we entertained one another with talent shows—singing, dancing, acting, reciting poetry. Most recently, I was reminded of these times looking at the faces of audiences watching that moment in the film *Four Weddings and a Funeral* when the grieving lover recites W. H. Auden's poem "Funeral Blues." My favorite verse proclaims: "He was my North, my South, my East and West, / My working week and my Sunday rest, / My noon, my midnight, my talk, my song, / I thought that love would last forever: I was wrong." Those words on paper are powerful. Yet spoken with passion, they are pure magic. They enable the listener to be moved, touched, taken to a place beyond words—transported.

Seduced by the magic of written and spoken words in childhood, I am still transported, carried away by writing and reading. Writing longhand the first drafts of all my work, I read aloud to myself. Performing the words to both hear and feel them, I want to be certain I am grappling with language in a manner where my words live and breathe, where they surface from a passionate place inside me. Had I entered my writing life as a critic, working in this way might not have mattered. Instead, I began writing poems. Standing in our living room, during dark southern nights when the earth was shaken by fierce thunderstorms and all electrical power was down, I performed, reciting poems, either those I had written or the works of favorite poets. During those strange and unpredictable nights I practiced the art of making words matter. In the stark daylight, I learned by heart the words that would be spoken in the shadows of candlelight, words that enchant, seduce—move. Long before criticism had any place in my mind and imagination, I had been taught in the segregated institutions of my childhood church and school that writing and performing should deepen the meaning of words, should illuminate, transfix, and transform.

Back then, I would have grieved deeply had any prophetic eye looked into the future and shared that I would one day become most well known as a critic, not as a writer of poetry or fiction. All the years I spent in college classes studying and reading literary criticism did nothing to convince me that writing criticism could be an act of passion. The criticism we were encouraged to write as students, that received affirmation and approval, sounded dead. However, it was likely to be held in higher esteem if it conveyed a lack of passionate engagement with words. This dispassionate stance was most often heralded as more objective. We were wrongly taught that it was an expression of neutrality. In actuality, it was an assertion of the hierarchical divide separating critic and writer. The critic, we learned, was superior to the writer. We also learned that this position of superiority sanctioned dominance, that it was accorded by virtue of location, by the critical act of looking over and down on the writer. It was the perfect metaphysical dualistic match of mind and body, with there being no doubt which was superior. In the university then, and often now, clear distinctions were made between writer and critic. There was no safe crossing of the boundaries separating the two. Reflecting on this artificial separation in *Voice Lessons: On Becoming a (Woman) Writer*, Nancy Mairs declares: "I believe in the reality of work. Period. I do not distinguish betwen creative and critical writing because all writing is creative. . . . And all writing is critical, requiring the same shifting, selection, scrutiny and judgement of the material at hand. The distinctions are not useful except to people who want to engender an other with whom they can struggle and over whom they can gain power. And because they are useful in that way, they are dangerous. . . ." Refusing to accept these distinctions was and remains a rebellious act, one that can challenge and disrupt hierarchical structures rooted in a politics of domination both within the academy and in the world outside.

That refusal demarcates. It separates those of us who choose to write as a vocation rather than as an academic practice. All academics write but not all see themselves as writers. Writing to fulfill professional career expectations is not the same as writing that emerges as the fulfillment of a yearning to work with words when there is no clear benefit or reward, when it is the experience of writing that matters. When writing is a desired and accepted calling, the writer is devoted, constant, and committed in a manner that is akin to monastic spiritual practice. I am driven to write, compelled by a constant longing to choreograph, to bring words together in patterns and configurations that move the spirit. As a writer, I seek that moment of ecstasy when I am dancing with words, moving in a circle of love so complete that like the mystical dervish who dances to be one with the Divine, I move toward the infinite. That fulfillment can be realized whether I write poetry, a play, fiction, or critical essays.

My fifteen published books are all works of nonfiction, most of them collections of critical essays. Turning to the short essay form was part of a revolt against the graduate-school tradition of writing the long-winded padded paper. To me the critical essay is the most useful form for the expression of a dialectical engagement with ideas that begins in my head, in my talking back to the books I am reading. It is also a way to extend the conversations I have with other critical thinkers. When I begin writing a critical essay, it is never the starting point for any discussion; it emerges as the site of culmination or a location for prolonged engagement, an invitation to work in a sustained manner with ideas. Since the critical essay can be read in a shorter amount of time than a book, and read again and again, it can offer a body of ideas that the critic and reader can grapple with, come back to. Nancy Mairs's assertion that she chooses the essay "for its power to both focus and disrupt" resonates with me. The critical essay demands the articulation of an agenda. It is a space where one writes to take a stand, to express and reveal points of view that are particular, specific, and directed—a great place to "throw down," to confront, interrogate, provoke.

At the heart of the critical essay is an engagement with ideas, with a contemplative realm of thought that is not passive but active. Michel Foucault evokes that active stance in the epigraph to *Language, Counter-Memory, Practice* with the insistence that this

active engagement with ideas emerges first in critical thinking: "Thought is no longer theoretical. As soon as it functions it
offends or reconciles, attracts or repels, breaks, dissociates, unites or
reunites; it cannot help but liberate and enslave. Even before pre-
scribing, suggesting a future, saying what must be done, even
before exhorting or merely sounding an alarm, thought, at the level
of its existence, in its very dawning, is in itself an action—a perilous
act." When such thought evolves into a body of ideas in a critical
essay that sense of provocation and peril is intensified. A seductive
atmosphere of pleasure and danger surrounds the writing process.
As a writer, intellectual, and critical thinker, I feel swept away by
the process of thinking through certain ideas as well as by their
potential to incite and arouse the reader.

Since many of the critical essays I write are used in classroom settings, I often receive tremendous critical feedback about the work,
both positive and negative. It was this feedback that intensified my
awareness of the power of the essay. A short piece of critical writing
can be easily shared (faxed or photocopied). This accessibility makes
it a marvelous catalyst for critical exchange that is different from
the collective reading of a book. Initially, professors were usually
the individuals who shared that a group of students who might
not have spoken much about assigned work in a class would be
intensely provoked to talk among themselves about an essay I had
written. Then I began to hear from other readers. Students shared
their pleasure at reading theoretical work that is clear and succinct.
Sometimes parents tell me about reading an essay with their children. Women who have been battered, who live for a time or work
in shelters, talk and write to me about discussing my work in their
groups. One of my favorite critical responses came from an incarcer-
ated black man who shared that the essays I write on sexism were
the catalyst for much critical discussion among his peers, so much

so that he declared, "Your name has become a household word around this prison." I write with the intent to share ideas in a manner that makes them accessible to the widest possible audience. This means that I often engage in a thinking and writing process where I am pushing myself to work with ideas in a way that strips them down, that cuts to the chase and does not seek to hide or use language to obscure meaning. The longing to pattern the words and ideas so that they are "in your face"—so that they have an immediacy, a clarity that need not be searched for, that is present right now—allows me to transfer to the act of writing vernacular modes of verbal exchange that surface in the expressive culture of the southern black working class.

In my own imagination, this process of thinking and writing is affirmed by the Buddhist vision of interior arrangement, where one strives to create a particular atmosphere with aesthetic minimalism, with an eye for simplicity. The point is not to render ideas less complex—the point is to make the complex clear. The outcome should be that the difficult terrain of thought traversed that has enabled one to arrive at certain standpoints or conclusions is not evident. Like too much clutter, it has been cleared away to make that which is most significant more apparent. In her discussion of "Theory's Contemplative Relation to the World," Joan Cocks speaks of critical theorizing and writing as a process that reveals "an intrinsic passion for the perverse revelation." We write "to find secrets in experience that are obscured from ordinary sight: to uncover hidden coherences in what seems to be a mere jumble of unrelated events and details, and incoherences in what appears to be strictly ordered; to make transparent what is opaque, and to expose opacity in what seems transparent."

Deconstruction is a useful critical tool to use in this process because it makes essential understanding the multilayered structures that underlie particular discursive formations. Gayatri Spivak has spoken and written quite eloquently about the usefulness of deconstructive awareness as a standpoint that compels critical vigilance: "Deconstruction points out that in constructing any kind of an argument we must move from implied premises, that must necessarily obliterate or finesse certain possibilities that question the availability of these premises in an absolutely justifiable way. Deconstruction teaches us to look at these limits and questions." When deconstruction is seen as a tool and not an end in itself, it constructively imposes an incredibly rigorous will to examine, critique, and analyze that moves the insurgent critical thinker away from attachment to a particular rhetoric or set of critical paradigms that it is easy to be seduced into stating again and again. One of the primary challenges of critical theorizing is the inherent demand that ideas make as they act upon the critical mind, internally challenging the critic to be continually moving from fixed positions. To me that means that we are not just writing but changing the way we are writing given what we are saying and whom we hope to speak with and to. Spivak makes me laugh with recognition when she warns against intellectuals trying to "save the masses," speak for and describe them, urging us instead "to learn to speak in such a way that the masses will not regard as bullshit." When critics write to engage wider diverse audiences, we confront the limitations of discourse, of the languages we use. It becomes ruthlessly apparent that unless we are able to speak and write in many different voices, using a variety of styles and forms, allowing the work to change and be changed by specific settings, there is no way to converse across borders, to speak to and with diverse communities.

Contemporary cultural critics, particularly those of us who write about popular culture, must be ever vigilant in our work because it is all too easy to end up writing in an ethnographic self-serving manner about topics that do not engage us in a sustained dialogue with the cultural producers and audiences providing us with the "texts" we discuss. This diminishes the power of our work to make meaningful critical interventions in theory and practice for anyone. As Joan Cocks reminds us in *The Oppositional Imagination*: "There can be a faddishness to theory, so that it pursues not the answers to difficult questions but the latest fashionable thinker or thought. It can lose connection altogether with the world and feed like a narcissist off its own concepts and principles." This is especially true of critical writing on popular culture because it has the appearance of immediacy, of direct contact and engagement. Often merely choosing to write about popular culture can carry with it the assumption that one is "down"—completed divested of attachment to notions of coercive hierarchy and politics of domination. Yet when privileged class groups write about the marginalized and disenfranchised this act alone is not a gesture of political solidarity. It can be as much an act of colonizing appropriation as the more apparent conventional modes of white supremacist capitalist patriarchal dominance.

Writing cultural criticism to be hip and cool, especially when the subject is popular culture, allows critics to indulge in acts of appropriation without risk. Fascinating, titillating cultural criticism that looks at the popular without engaging a radical or revolutionary political agenda really does not disrupt and challenge traditional uses of theory; it helps maintain the existing barriers and cultural hierarchies of domination. Critical writing counts for very little when critics speak about ending domination, eradicating racism, sexism (which includes the structure of heterosexism), class elitism in our work without changing individual habits of being, without allowing those ideas to work in our lives and on our souls in a manner that transforms.

To engage a politics of transformation we surrender the need to occupy a space of hedonistic intellectual "cool" that covertly embraces old notions of objectivity and neutrality. Certainly, I and my work are often seen as not cool enough precisely because there is always an insistence on framing ideas politically and calling for active resistance. A lot of new fashionable cultural criticism, whether it is postcolonial, multicultural, queer theory, or some combination of categories, gains a hearing precisely because of the dissenting voices of intellectuals who were not and/or are not afraid to take political stands in our work even though we risk being dismissed as not being theoretical "enough," intellectual "enough." And it should not surprise anyone that it is often the "cool" cultural critics who both labor in the academy and depend on its structures of valuation for regard and reward who most invest in the production of new hierarchies that still keep in place patterns of coercive competition and domination. A really good example of this tendency is a lot of the critical writing that intellectual elites of all races do that focuses on underclass and poor black experience. It is as though black popular culture has become the latest frontier to be colonized, occupied, and made over in the interests of the colonizer. Being "down" does not mean that any of us have surrendered our will to colonize.

As a cultural worker on the left, I labor to critically think and write in a manner that clearly names the concrete strategies for radical and/or revolutionary interventions I use in everyday life to resist politics of domination. As a conscious strategic choice, this practice makes it possible for my life and work to embody a politics of transformation that addresses the concerns of individuals and communities in resistance. This means that the work of critical thinking and theorizing is itself an expression of political praxis that constructs a foundation wherein individual action can be united with collective struggle. The mutual interplay between critic and reader is a site for contestation and confrontation. It calls us to be critically aware, to not become lazy or sloppy in our thinking.

Dissenting critical voices are easily co-opted by the longing to be both heard and admired, our words longed for and affirmed. Subculture stardom can be as seductive a distraction as speaking in the interests of mainstream cultural politics of domination. Critical writing that remains on the edge, able to shift paradigms, to move in new directions, subverts this tendency. It demands of critics fundamental intellectual allegiance to radical openness, to free thinking. In *Technical Difficulties*, June Jordan declares, "If you are free, you are not predictable and you are not controllable." I was reminded of this recently when I was not invited to a conference celebrating and critically engaging the work of my close comrade Cornel West. When I asked an "insider" why I was excluded I was told, "You insist on being an independent thinker. You're a 'wild card.' No one knows what you will say. You're too unpredictable." My presence would have threatened presumably because it was feared that I might be critical of West's work and thought. Exclusion and isolation, whether they occur through overt or covert acts, have always been useful tactics of terrorism, a powerful way to coerce individuals to conform, to change. No insurgent intellectual, no dissenting critical voice in this society escapes the pressure to conform. This is especially true of any dissenting voice that remains within a hierarchial institution founded on structures of domination where rewards and benefits are awarded in relation to service rendered. However, irrespective of our locations, we are all vulnerable. We can all be had, co-opted, bought. There is no special grace that rescues any of us. There is only a constant struggle to keep the faith, to relentlessly rejoice in an engagement with critical ideas that is itself liberatory, a practice of freedom.

That moment when I whirl with words, when I dance in that ecstatic circle of love surrounded by ideas, is a space of transgression. There are no binding limitations; everything can be both held and left behind—race, gender, class. It is this intensely intimate moment of passionate transcendence that is the experiential reality that deepens my commitment to a progressive politics of transformation. Writing these words, I look down at passages from the work of the Sufi mystic and poet Rumi taped to my desk. They challenge me: "Do you want the words or will you live what you know? Which is real, is it the theoretical knowledge? . . . Do you want the words or will you live what you know?" I write to live.

writing without labels

When I was a girl longing to be a writer, the writer whose work touched my soul, reaching into the innermost places where much within me had gone unrecognized and unloved, was Emily Dickinson. Even though I had my card game Authors, which gave me a visual portrait of her, I never saw her as a white woman. Reading her work I never thought about race or sex. Even though I was stealing away to the privacy of our attic rooms to hold her words close in a real world of racial apartheid that affected my life daily, determining even where I could walk and eat and sit (the colored-only section at the movie theater), when it came to words on the page all this was forgotten. Intuitively, I understood that the persona of the writer was not as important as the words that grip, hold, and transform. I read other women writers. Their work did not speak to me. Clearly, I had not chosen Emily Dickinson because she had been born woman. Her vision resonated with mine. She evoked those emotions I felt but could not talk about with anyone. It was all there in her words.

The girl I was who longed to be a writer had been well schooled in the belief that art transcends categories. In our black segregated schools we never made a writer's race primary. It was always the work that mattered. Even if it was noted that we should give special attention to Langston Hughes's work because he was writing about a world we knew intimately, we also knew that shared racial identity and even common experience would not lead one to produce great writing. To become a great writer one had to be able to move deep into experience, into emotion, into life. Dickinson's field of vision made contemplation of metaphysics, of religion and nature the space where she experienced life to the fullest. While her race, gender, and class had shaped the outer boundaries of her experience, inside she lived unbounded. She lived in service to the imagination. She had surrendered. That was the mark of the great writer: the willingness to surrender to the power of the imagination.

When I begin writing poetry in girlhood utterly under the influence of William Wordsworth, Gerard Manley Hopkins, and Emily Dickinson, I dwelled only on the big issues, the universal concerns of life—death, love, sorrow, joy. Writing was a place where I could leave behind the ordinary mundane pain of my life. Imagination allowed me to move through and beyond this pain. I did not want writing to be the place where I told my story, where I confessed—I wanted it to be the paradise where I could forget the daily experiences that led me to certain emotional states. It was the emotional state that was the place where the imagination would find its treasures, not concrete experience. This is the reason I did not focus too intently on race, gender, or class.

In the realm of the concrete I did confront being black, female, and working class. I confronted it in the privacy of a domestic world where my longing to read these poets from another time and far-away places was not fully understood. I confronted it all the more when I let it be known that I wanted to become a writer. No one tried to dissuade me from writing; they simply talked about what I would do to make a living. Writing, in their eyes, could be done when one came home from work. It was not that they did not respect writing. It was that they saw it as having nothing to do with real life. To everyone in our world words on paper were magical. They filled me and those around me with awe. Even then I understood that doing the real work of the imagination required time—space to dream, contemplate, and talk with spirits, space to prepare oneself for the sacred rite of putting words on paper. I was not at all interested in making a living. I thought then that my destiny could be just like Emily Dickinson's. I could stay alone in my little house and write. Of course as a young girl believing in magic I did not think in concrete terms about how I would acquire the house, the means to survive. I thought it would happen like magic. I let no one dissuade me from my dream of becoming a writer.

I held on to that dream even as the concrete world of race, class, and gender begin to impinge upon that imaginary space I created for myself where all was possible. In the all-black schools of my childhood there had never been any doubt that we had equal access to the world of the imaginary. No teacher had ever looked upon my love of reading and my longing to write with scorn, ridicule, or contempt. No one had ever suggested that being black, female, or working-class would stand in my way. No wonder then that I cherish the memory of those all-black schools where no one ever thought my love of Dickinson and Wordsworth was strange, where no one ever questioned my right to love great literature no matter who had written it. Racial desegregation changed all that. In the white school smart black people were suspect. Even though my teachers nurtured my longing to write, it was there that I first learned that I would confront barriers—that there would be folks who would not be able to take writing by a black author seriously.

In high school, I began my search for black writers. To this day I remember the incredible sense of ecstasy that I felt when I first found an edited volume of poetry by black writers. There in that slim little book I read sonnets by Countee Cullen and Claude McKay. I read the short beautiful poems of Georgia Douglas Johnson, a kindred spirit who I knew in my heart must have read and loved Dickinson as I read and loved her. Finding the work of these black poets affirmed that I was not a freak, a special aberration. It was so inspiring. It is truly difficult to find words that will adequately convey what it was like to suddenly be forced to study in a world of white authority figures challenging everything about the world I had known before coming into their power. That white world made me doubt myself. And in the space of that doubt I needed proof that they were all wrong—that there are great writers who happened to be black, just as my beloved Emily Dickinson happened to be white. Despite the fact that it was hard to find published writings by black authors, I found my proof and I was set free.

I often think about this time in my life when I hear contemporary debates about whether the identity of the writer matters. Rarely are those who want to insist that it is only great literature that matters willing to acknowledge that in a culture defined and organized around principles of race, gender, and class domination, identity matters simply because structures that silence and shut out are already in place to assault the consciousness of anyone who dares to live by the belief that we are always more than labels. It was not the world of segregated blackness that sought to deny me a place of transcendence where the content of my writing would be deemed more important than the color of my skin. The world of whiteness imposed rigid barriers. The logic of that world, of white supremacy, had to be resisted. To the extent that I was always struggling against racism, race mattered. Making sure that it did not become the issue that mattered most or the only issue that mattered was the burden placed on me. Assimilating into mainstream white culture would have been the easiest way to flee these difficulties. I could simply live as though I were white. Issues of race and racism could be conveniently ignored or dismissed as irrelevant. One of my favorite writers, Jean Toomer, had tried to escape the burden of racial identity by passing. Ironically, this choice blocked and deadened his creative imagination.

When I am at my desk writing, I always think of myself as a writer who is a black woman. I never think: I am a black woman writer. Race and gender are made to come first in the world outside, where if one is from a marginalized group anything about you that does not conform to white male norms is acknowledged first and foremost. Even when a black and/or woman writer is praised for not calling attention to race or gender, these categories are still being highlighted. Deviance from expectation is no escape. Writers from marginalized groups are usually faced with two options: overidentification with an identity or disidentification. In actuality our realities encompass the complexity of being both a writer in the best and most transcendent understanding of that vocation and being individuals whose work is informed by the specifics of race, class, and gender. William Faulkner is a traditionally accepted "great" writer who is one of my favorites. As a professor of American literature talking about his work I usually emphasize the larger themes of that work: death and dying, lost love, failure to achieve desired dreams. Yet there would be no way to adequately talk about his vision without also acknowledging that the perspective of the fictional South he created was definitely shaped by his race, gender, and class. Clearly, those identifying labels matter; the fact is they do not matter in some absolute way. Writers who seek to flee any reference to identifying labels of race, gender, class, or sexual practice often do so because the tendency is to make too much of them. Yet to act as though they have no importance whatsoever denies all of us the opportunity to have an expansive understanding of the influences and passions at work in the writer's imagination.

In her nonfiction British writer Jeanette Winterson goes to great pains to disassociate herself from the label "lesbian writer." Positively, she endeavors to lay claim again and again to that space of creativity where any committed artist is more concerned with the work than with identities sexual or otherwise. In "The Semiotics of Sex" she declares: "I am a writer who happens to love women. I am not a lesbian who happens to write." However, while she goes to great pains to critique gay thinkers for acting as though sexual identity is important, she does not painstakingly critique heterosexist thinkers for refusing to approach work that focuses on differences in an unbiased manner. Sound and beautiful writing is not the only reason Jeanette Winterson's work found both acclaim and a sustained audience. Were it not for the activism preceding the publication of work like hers challenging heterosexism, done by individuals who openly identify as gay and by their allies in struggle, there might not have been any mainstream audience, however large or small, capable of appreciating Winterson's work. While she is right to castigate any individual who approaches her and the work concerned only with what she or any writer is doing sexually, she oversimplifies the issue when she implies that no mention should be made of homosexuality.

At no point does Winterson suggest that writers should not be required to speak about their sexuality. Such thinking would not curry favor with mainstream critics. No one would balk at a critical reader of the work of Henry Miller or Norman Mailer, both white heterosexual male writers, who made reference to their autobiographical comments about their sexuality. Indeed, these comments illuminate the work. At times it appears that Winterson objects to any mention of sexuality if a writer is gay. Any writer should resist any attempt to see their work solely as a reflection of one aspect of who they are.

Winterson is on target when she insists that "to continue to ask someone about their homosexuality, when the reason to talk is a book, a picture, a play, is harassment by the back door." Yet at times it seems that she wishes to deny that sexual practice in any way influences work. Her comments are mere mimicry of the elitist tone of generations of white male writers and critics who though writing very specific and autobiographically based work insisted that it was always and only universal. In fact, really great writing is usually both specific and universal in its appeal. Winterson's comments often seem to be oriented towards currying favor from a mainstream traditional critical public. With heavy-handed didacticism she contends: "Art must resist autobiography if it hopes to cross boundaries of class, culture . . . and . . . sexuality. Literature is not a lecture delivered to a special interest group, it is a force that unites its audience. The sub-groups are broken down." Does Winterson seriously believe that centuries of heterosexual writers never included openly gay characters in their fictions because they were resisting autobiography? The truth is heterosexuality was infinitely more familiar to them. To the extent that they were writing from a foundation of what they knew, they were writing autobiographically. It is utterly pretentious and false for any writer to act as though only gay writers, and writers from other marginal groups, have indulged in merely describing their reality. There is infinitely more autobiographically based bad writing published by heterosexual writers. The desire on the part of any writer from a marginalized group to emphasize the aspect of their reality that has previously been aggressively denied as a result of political repression is natural. And even though a consequence of this may be that the reading public is often offered writing from that group which is shallow, poorly crafted, or sensational, the breaking down of social barriers that once precluded the telling of such stories makes it all the more possible for great writing to emerge. When writers from marginalized groups do work that is truly marvelous, this writing is not seen by dominant audiences as personifying the group's capabilities. Usually it is seen as a rare exception. Yet if there is a marvelous book by a straight white male writer and ten trashy books by the same, this group's capability will be judged by the better work.

Ironically, the power of great writing by a writer from a marginalized group to inspire and influence the work of emerging writers from that group is diminished when such an individual disassociates their work from that of peers from similar circumstances. Concurrently, this disassociation tends to reinscribe the assumption, rooted in already existing biases, that this writing and the writer represents an exception. Individual writers from marginal groups often invest in the idea of their specialness. They may feel threatened when aspiring writers seek to do equally compelling work. Black writers often feel pitted against one another, especially for attention from white-dominated mass media. When planning the marketing of my most recent memoir, a white woman publicist commented that I might have difficulty getting reviews in publications because another black woman writer was publishing a memoir at the same time. My first response was to call attention to the fact that at least six white women writers had published memoirs at the same time and magazines had no trouble focusing on all of them, sometimes in articles that addressed their work individually and at other times collectively. She agreed that this had happened but that "it just does not work that way for black writers." Again it is not the black writer seeking to ghettoize but rather the racial biases of mainstream white press that make it evident by such practices that only one of us at a time can expect to receive attention.

To counter racist agendas at both the editorial and public-relations level, I fantasize, as many writers do, of writing a book where no mention is made of my race or gender—where the work has to be considered on its own terms. To fantasize this is to imagine a publishing world that no longer exists, if it ever did. Now more than ever the persona of the writer is as much a feature of marketing strategy as is the work's content. Doris Lessing exposed this when she tried several years ago to get a book published using a pseudonym. The manuscript deemed worthless and discarded when seen as written by a nobody was eagerly snapped up when Lessing revealed she was the writer. Whether the labels attached to writers and marketed are identifiers of race, sex, or some other characteristic that sets the individual apart from others, it is always limiting to be defined by one aspect of one's identity.

The black and/or female writer who publishes work that specifically focuses on race or gender issues will often find that their writing on all other subjects will be ignored. To be labeled the "feminist" writer means one is likely to be excluded from any acknowledgment that you are someone capable of writing about topics that extend beyond this marker. Equally so, to approach feminist publishing with the desire to do work that does not "fit" with the prevailing tone and temper of the movement is to also be excluded. Even though we are living in a time when the rhetoric of the house embraces multiculturalism and diversity, writers who are not straight white males who resist confinement to any category or subject matter in their work often find themselves reinscribed into limiting confined spaces by mass media. Unfortunately, the language of mass media is not a rhetoric of complexity; the more complex the vision the harder it is to convey in a short interview, brief comment, or book review. When a writer has a body of work the critical reader may only have looked at the one book they are discussing but on the basis of this one text will assume that they fully comprehend the scope of the author's concern. The more marginal one's group status in the culture, the less likely work will be given serious attention by mainstream media. Often press who are hostile to feminism deny any woman writer with this label attached to her work quality time or attention. As a black woman professor and writer who writes about the politics of representation, I am well aware of the extent to which white women readers are seen by the mainstream media as the only meaningful audience for writing by and about women. As a consequence, if a black woman writer writes work that specifically addresses black female experience, the tacit assumption will be that the work has no appeal for white females. However, it is always assumed that books written by white females specifically about their experience have universal appeal.

As a reader I find I am wholeheartedly able to identify with work by white women even when it does not address the experiences I am most familiar with. For example: Erica Jong's witty autobiographical account of aging, *Fear of Fifty,* highlights growing up white and Jewish. Her personal stories delight me even though our backgrounds are in no way similar. The difficulty lies with mass media not realizing that white women readers are interested in work by black women. This is especially true of mass-market women's magazines. Of course only white women writers can write about their specific experiences without ever having to describe themselves as white. When I first published my memoir, *Bone Black,* I kept describing it as a memoir about girlhood that emphasizes growing up black and southern, among other experiences. Again and again editors tried to describe it solely as a memoir about black girlhood. I resisted this so as not to imply that nonblack women could not relate to the experiences I recall. The large number of letters I received from white women readers who identified with the experiences I shared was yet another reminder of how empathy allows us to understand another's differences.

If all writers consciously used identifying labels in ways that describe without defining we would be able to see the larger picture both in relation to an author's vision and her personal story. In the case of Jeanette Winterson, I read her work before hearing any information about her person, her nationality, race, class background, or sexual practice. Later I was pleased to learn that she was from a rural working-class family that had difficulty accepting her love of reading because that is an experience akin to my own. No large numbers of successful writers come from working-class rural backgrounds. The extent to which that formative experience shapes a writer's vision fascinates me. I can value this bit of information without allowing it to overdetermine my reading of her work.

In all my years of writing I have never heard any writer from a marginalized group insist that readers should only read gay writers if they are gay, black straight writers if they are black and straight. I do not know where to find writers who are so attached to labels. I hear about them most in the works of conservative thinkers who are condemning their narrowmindedness, their failure to understand that great literature transcends race and gender. In her collection of essays *Skin: Talking About Sex, Class and Literature*, Dorothy Allison shares again and again that her work as an activist for lesbian and feminist movement never led her to assume that she would write from a limited perspective. To her and fellow lesbians whose writing she admires, "literature was about refusing all categories." Allison remembers one of her teachers, Bertha Harris, declaring: "There is no lesbian literature, she told us. The relevant word was literature, real literature that came out of an authentic lesbian culture." Concurrently, there is no black literature, only literature that conveys our experience as black people. There is no feminist writer, only the writer who writes from a feminist perspective.

I and all the writers I know want to be respected first and foremost for our work; the root meaning of the word *respect* is "to look at." Writing can be considered on its own terms and then it can also be looked at in relation to a writer's background and personal history. My experience as a southern working-class black female from a religious family has shaped the way I see the world. Yet the specificity of that experience does not keep me from addressing universal concerns. It is not an either/or issue and never has been. Both in our past and present the tyranny of race, gender, and social biases has meant that disenfranchised writers have had to struggle for voice and recognition in ways that highlight identity. That struggle has not ended, as we must now resist the form recognition takes when these categories are then deployed to confine and restrict our voices. If long-standing structures of hierarchy and domination were not still in place and daily reinscribed, calling attention to a writer's race, gender, class, or sexual practice would illuminate work, expand awareness and understanding. I am not a writer who happens to be black. I am a writer who is black and female. These aspects of my identity strengthen my creative gifts. They are neither burdens nor limitations. By fully embracing all the markers that situate and locate me, I know who I am. Writing the truth of what we know is the essence of all great and good literature.

writing to confess

When I was a girl obsessed with reading biographies and auto-biographies more than twenty years ago, the vast majority of the works I read were by and about white males. The book that most influenced my consciousness of writing during my early teens was Rilke's *Letters to a Young Poet*. This book entered the closed, racially segregated world of my upbringing by a very serendipitous and circuitous route. I had become involved with a racially integrated group of Christians who were actively involved in Campus Crusade for Christ. While my parents were religious and basically fundamentalist in their religious beliefs they were suspicious of overzealous participation in cult-like Christian groups. Not only did they try to limit my involvement with the well-meaning but "crazy" white folks who were leading this movement, they were vehemently opposed to progressive interpretations of Scriptures and the new biblical texts that they saw as blasphemous interpretations of the Word. And more than anything they mistrusted ecumenical approaches to religious worship. Hence their reluctance to let me attend a spiritual retreat in the hills of Tennessee. I remember my incessant crying and pleading, the intensity of their refusal, but I cannot recall their reasons for changing their minds. I do know that one of the good "crazy" folks had spoken with them and assured them that I would not be seduced away from the faith of my home church.

At this spiritual retreat I was seduced by the talks given by a progressive Catholic priest. For many of us lost and tormented souls he provided spiritual guidance. He listened to my dreams of wanting to be a writer, of feeling always like an outsider, a freak especially at home with family, and he comforted me. Sensing my despair with life, he sent to me one of the progressive young white women students who was part of his campus fellowship. I was sitting in a corner on the floor by a window that sunny day, looking out on the hills, feeling the heat as comfort and sanctuary. The sight brought to mind the passage "I will lift up my eyes unto the hills— from whence cometh my help." When she joined me, this student of the priest, who was beautiful and ethereal in her presence, giving me a hug and talking in hushed tones about writing, she carried in her hand a parting gift. It was her worn, tattered copy of Rilke's *Letters to a Young Poet*. In the memoir of my girlhood, *Bone Black*, I say of this book: "Rilke gives meaning to the wilderness of spirit I am living in. His book is a world I enter and find myself. I read *Letters to a Young Poet* over and over again. I am drowning and it is the raft that takes me safely to the shore."

When Rilke's work entered my life it brought me joy and a vision of artistic freedom. His whiteness and maleness were not foregrounded, nor was his German identity. Of course I recognized these identity markers but I was engaged with the ideas he offered. I have never heard any critic belittling the confessional nature of these letters. Diverse readers seem to all agree that these letters have enriched our understanding of writing, of creative process. In recent years as women of all races/ethnicities and men of color embrace confessional writing as a way of coming to voice, whether through autobiographies, memoirs, letters, diaries, etc., mainstream critics aggressively devalue such writing. As an undergraduate student at Stanford University at the peak of contemporary feminist movement, it was thrilling to be in classrooms where critical interventions were being made that allowed for the reclamation of writing by women that had been lost because of patriarchal culture's devaluation of women's words. In those classrooms I and other students were not only taught that we should strive to be excellent thinkers and writers, we were taught to value good writing whether it was done by women or men. In recent years, antifeminist backlash constructs a monolithic feminist classroom where all students are taught to hate work by men, to have no aesthetic standards, no appreciation for "great" literature. This was not my experience nor has it been the experience of most of my students.

Feminist insistence that "the personal is political" did encourage many women to engage in existential self-reflection about the meaning of life, especially in relation to sexism and male domination. That critical exploration created a renaissance in women's autobiographical writing. Much of this writing was not exceptional. Yet its lack of literary merit was not due to the confessional dimension but rather lack of skills, etc. Not all the women who began writing for the first time as a consequence of engagement in feminist movement were engaged with the craft of writing. Many of these women did not want to be "writers," but they did want to document their lives. The growing body of confessional writing by women coincided with the proliferation in mass culture of the talk show as a place for personal confession. Since these shows are designed to appeal to a predominately female market many of the topics for discussion are appropriated from cultural narratives that were initially validated only within feminist circles, narratives about child abuse, domestic violence, rape, sexual harassment, abortion, etc. Patriarchal mass media's appropriation and popularization of these topics helped create a cultural context where the confessional narrative has been trivialized, made to appear solely a gesture that is self-serving and exhibitionist. This trivialization has led to an overall devaluation of any confessional narrative.

In actuality, writers who make use of personal confession do not share a common style, standpoint, or intent. This is as true for women writers as men. Yet sexism tends to ensure that women's writing is often approached as though it is all the same—every woman speaking through one voice. Concurrently, in some feminist circles there is both a tendency to ignore the differences in women's writing as well as a desire to disregard aesthetic considerations that would lead the work of some writers to be valued more than others. While I was educated as a student of literature in my undergraduate years and in graduate school to believe that standards are important, that I should strive to attain literary excellence in my writing, there were other women coming to voice in places both inside and outside the academy who were learning to question the notion of standards. In the essay "Believing in Literature" Dorothy Allison recalls the confusion she felt when she was taught to question literary canons in ways that suggested there was no standard for aesthetic evaluation. In the particular feminist world she inhabited women were, to some extent, "making an ethical system that insists a lightweight romance has the same worth as a serious piece of fiction, that there is no good or bad, no 'objective' craft or standards of excellence." Significantly, among women, those of us who were striving to be writers before we were actively engaged in contemporary feminist movement always insisted on the importance of craft and standards, resisting notions that all women's voices were "equal." We brought this insistence on the importance of standards into feminist writing even though such thinking was often at odds with the perspective that the only act that was important was women coming to voice in writing. Differences in perspective were also influenced by whether women came to writing outside the academy or inside. The emphasis on breaking silences in contemporary feminist movement led women to create journal-writing workshops and diverse conventional and unconventional creative-writing seminars that urged women to write. Certainly those of us who were working to earn doctorates in traditional English departments would not have been able to attain our degrees if we had not recognized the importance of aesthetic standards both in relation to our work and to evaluating the work of our peers and students. Whenever mainstream critics critique feminist influence on women's writing they tend to ignore the differences and to act as though feminist movement can always be best understood by focusing on its most unproductive elements. In recent years, conservative antifeminist backlash has painted a portrait of women's studies and feminist movement that suggests there is a total lack of concern among women writers for standards and literary excellence.

Significantly, feminist questioning of the gender and race biases in established literary canons did lead to important rethinking of how we might create standards for literary excellence and/or use traditional modes of evaluation in ways that would not reinscribe existing structures of domination. These critical interventions were crucial for everyone. They were especially inspiring to women and men from marginal groups who were striving to become writers in a culture that had heretofore only valued the voices of privileged white male writers and the rare token white female or female and male of color. Concurrently, the fact that feminist emphasis on excavating the personal as a way to understand our political locations enabled many of us to break with traditional academic training, which had taught many of us to believe that work was objective and neutral if we did not overtly refer to the personal or even use the word *I*. We learned to critically interrogate the notion of objectivity. We learned to see that every work conveyed a political standpoint even if it was covertly embedded in the text. We learned to understand the ways language that was taught to us as "neutral" usually reflected the prevailing hierarchies of race and gender. All of these interventions helped many women let go of years of being taught that we could not be good writers and/or that writing from a clear politics of location wherein one did not attempt to appear neutral but rather overtly identified standpoint, perspective, agenda, and political concerns was as valuable as other types of writing.

There is no doubt that in some case feminist thinkers overvalued the "personal" and made it seem that any confessional statement however trite or meaningless was important. Yet these errors of judgment, which may have led to an increase in "bad" confessional writing, were part of a constructive process wherein the field of creativity was expanded. More women than ever before could explore the terrain of writing. More voices could be heard. Many of us were inspired. Our confidence in ourselves was strengthened and our devotion to the craft of writing deepened. Addressing the power of this movement essayist Nancy Mairs exclaimed in *Voice Lessons*: "In fact, the autobiographical pitch and timbre distinguishing this voice that utters me developed unconsciously but not spontaneously during the years after finding community under the pear trees, when, as a doctoral student, I began at last to attend seriously to the words and intonations of women as women. I found my writing voice, and go on finding it, in precisely the same way that I came to my first utterances: by listening to the voices around me. . . ." To find a writing voice many women had to hear themselves through the act and art of confession.

Unfortunately, as conflicts among feminist thinkers intensified, particularly debate over the nature and direction of feminist theory, the political and theoretical arguments underpinning the notion that the personal is political were forgotten. Within feminist circles individuals began to critique and ridicule any emphasis on personal confession. Ironically, despite the absence of a sustained mass-based feminist movement addressing a large body of women and men, feminist theory that was metalinguistic, abstract, and very difficult to comprehend was more valued than any work that endeavored to address a larger audience. Collective feminist failure to stand by the principle of exploring the personal while simultaneously upholding literary standards when it came to the craft of writing helped diminish the value and significance of the personal as a site for existential reflection. Even though women from all backgrounds continued to tell their stories, eventually there was little or no critical recognition of the ways writers deployed the confessional narrative with diverse intentionality. Writers who valued confession narratives whose work was most linked to feminist politics and feminist theory could not count on critical readers, especially reviewers, to take note of issues of style, content, or purpose. Indeed it was much more likely that such writing would be dismissed without careful literary evaluation.

When I first began writing feminist theory I did not include personal confession. I began to use confessional anecdotes as a strategy to engage diverse readers. Coming from a black working-class background, I was especially concerned with the importance of creating liberatory feminist theory that would speak to as many folks as possible. Through lectures and conversations I found that audiences across race and class were quite willing to engage complex theoretical issues if they were presented in ways that were accessible. Using an anecdotal story to illustrate an idea was one way to bridge the gap between feminist thinking emerging from university settings and the more common discourses of gender taking place in everyday life.

As my academic writing received public attention, I was not represented in published discussions of my work as a writer who also did feminist theory. My public reputation was based solely on academic writing. While I had not wished it to be so, my writing had become more compartmentalized. Those individuals who were familiar with my work prior to my engagement in feminism saw me as an aspiring creative writer, working mostly to write poetry and fiction. They knew that I was committed to writing as a craft. The critical standards that I brought initially to creative writing served me well when I began writing literary criticism, feminist theory, and cultural criticism. I had been so well socialized by graduate school that I was torn between which writing path to pursue, agonizing over whether or not I could write from various standpoints in various genres. In part, my conventional academic training had encouraged me to believe that no writer could write well in various genres.

Within academic settings finding one's voice was often made synonymous with choosing a specific style and genre. As I began to write successfully in various genres I interrogated this notion of voice, embracing the reality that we can approach a subject from multiple standpoints using a variety of writing styles. Feminist thinking not only urged women to break traditional allegiance to genres; it also legitimized interdisciplinary work as well. However, my desire to bring to bear the standards I had learned in creative-writing classes to the writing of a dissertation and later to scholarly work was consistently seen as suspect by professors. It seemed as though one's intellectual ability was perceived as lacking if one remained concerned about writing style, about communicating in language in ways that were compelling. Eventually I let go of conventional thinking about genres, no longer accepting the idea that critical writing could not be creative, even though I had to continually confront a literary world that did not consider writing style that important when it came to academic work, particularly feminist writing. Academics who write both scholarly and non-scholarly work often find it difficult to receive recognition for "creative" writing. I wholeheartedly embrace Nancy Mairs's declaration that we recognize writing to be a more inclusive terrain when she declares: "I believe in the reality of work. Period. I do not distinguish between creative and critical writing because all writing is creative. . . . Whatever the product—poem, story, essay, letter to lover, technical report—the problem is the same: the page is empty and will have to be filled. Out of nothing, something. And all writing is critical, requiring the same sifting, selection, scrutiny, and judgment of the material at hand. The distinctions are not useful. . . ." Contemporary feminist movement enabled many of us to let go these distinctions and do all our writing work more creatively.

Feminist insistence that "the personal is political" certainly paved the way for all readers, not just women, to explore and value the confessional narrative. Oftentimes women tell their personal stories solely as an act of resistance, to break silences. At times these stories may be simply narcissistic, providing the reader with no complex understanding of the significance of a particular confession. The writer may show no interest in craft. Interviewed in *The Power to Dream*, a collection about women writers and their work, Maxine Hong Kingston shares her belief that "there are writers who give you life whether or not they write well." This has not been my experience. In my English classes I encourage all my students to appreciate writing that is well crafted and to seek to be skillful writers who worship at the throne of language. When writing personal narratives I urge them not to be self-indulgent, to refuse to be exhibitionist—to consider ways that they can best use language to convey various truths.

I am most interested in confessional writing when it allows us to move into the personal as a way to go beyond it. In all my work I evoke the personal as a prelude. It functions as a welcoming gesture, offering the reader a sense of who I am, a sense of location. Reader response to my theoretical work, the feminist theory and/or cultural criticism, lets me know how much this strategy empowers them. They respond to open, honest personal revelations and to the clarity of writing style. In writing memoirs, journals, and letters I also endeavor to make use of the personal for purposes that extend beyond mere description of self-indulgent revelation. For example: I wrote about my girlhood as a way to chart my development as an intellectual. As I have become more well-known as a thinker and a writer I am often asked about the path that led me from a small-town working-class background into the academy. At a time when so many young folks, particularly African-Americans, from poor and working-class backgrounds feel ambivalent about reading and studying, I felt it would be useful for me to share in print how much books were a force enabling me to realize my dreams. To me the writing of this memoir was like drawing a map. The journey it charts may serve as inspiration and affirmation to aspiring writers coming from backgrounds where their desire to write is discouraged or not affirmed.

Throughout time confessional writing by white men has resonated with male and female readers of all races. I began this essay talking about the impact of Rilke's letters on my consciousness pre-

67

cisely because it is the primary example from my girlhood of a work that transformed my thinking about writing even as it affirmed my will to write. In *The Last Generation*, Cherrie Moraga urges us to celebrate confession. "All writing is confession. Confession masked and revealed in the voices and faces of our characters. All is hunger. The longing to be known fully and still loved. The admission of our own inherent vulnerability, our weakness, our tenderness of skin, fragility of heart, our overwhelming desire to be relieved of the burden of ourselves in the body of another, to be forgiven of our ultimate aloneness in the mystical body of a god or the common work of a revolution. These are human considerations that the best of writers presses her fingers upon." Feminist focus on confessional narratives forged a cultural context in which women's autobiographical writing both past and present could be given sustained acknowledgment and recognition. It would be a tremendous loss for contemporary writing if the misuses of confessional narratives led to ongoing devaluation of the form itself.

Every woman's confessional narrative has more meaningful power of voice when it is well crafted. Women should not be afraid to critique a lack of standards in writing by women. To indulge in praising writing that is not compelling, that has no literary merit, means that critics collude in setting a stage for the devaluation of women's words, for future silences. Women will continue to confess, to tell our stories with wild abandon and recklessness. Yet the proliferation of published confessional writing may not mean that we permanently establish our place as serious writers within this canon. To be serious we must dare to be critical of our urge to tell our stories, of the ways we tell them.

telling all

the politics of confession

Memoirs have always intrigued me. Contrary to those who mock it, confession is good for the soul. The confessional narrative can function in many different ways. Therapeutically it can be a way to recover a lost sense of self or a way to release the past. It can be purely documentary. It can be an inspirational guide for life's journey. And it can also be a gesture of unadulterated exhibitionism.

Long before Kathryn Harrison appeared on the scene, Anaïs Nin was the great high priestess of the latter. Girlfriend loved looking at herself in the mirror both in "real life" and in the images she created in her books. I have always been especially fond of the title *A Spy in the House of Love*. The most memorable line in the book is when the heroine exclaims: "I have never found a way to get what I wanted except by lies." Like Nin, Harrison writes romantically about her consensual incestuous romantic liaison with her dad. Yet ultimately she lacks Nin's courage. For when confronted with public interrogation of her work, Harrison engages in a pretty sensational form of gaslighting—only it is not another person she betrays but her own narrative. While the book is in no way written as the story of an incest survivor, in her public discussions of the book, especially when she is answering critics, Harrison often suggests that this is the essence of her text.

Anyone who has actually read the compelling, intense memoir *The Kiss* and finds the book satisfying on its own terms (many of the people who talked about the book did not read it) knows a significant aspect of the work is the story it tells of the young adult Harrison's consensual seduction by and love affair with her father. This is not the only story Harrison narrates, even though it is the primary one she and everyone else talks about. In the book words like *incest* and *abuse* (which are constantly evoked in interviews and reviews) never appear. The language Harrison uses to describe this dangerous liaison comes straight out of conventional well-crafted romantic sexual thrillers. Yet if one listens to what the author says in mass media you might come away thinking this is a book that tells the true story of a female surviving coercive father/daughter incest. However, this book is not written as a survivor's confession nor is it a record of coercive abuse.

Harrison wants to have it all. She has chosen to write a sensational book that suggests that it is possible to have a consensual tortuous love affair as an adult woman with one's father and live to triumphantly tell the tale, yet simultaneously she seeks to gain recognition for being yet another abused female victim of a male oppressor. At times in the book, she blurs the line between defenseless girlhood and adult female agency. To escape censure from readers, at difficult moments in the narrative Harrison relies on representing herself as the little girl who just could not say no to daddy.

When daddy first sticks his tongue in his grown daughter's mouth she not only has a clue that this ain't right, she has the good sense to talk about it with her boyfriend. How she moves from this mature healthy response to the position of little Lolita who just can't say no is not made evident, for suddenly she retreats back into psychic girlhood. She may be an adult traveling by car and plane to get to that motel where she's doing it for daddy, but when she arrives on the scene she's just a little girl frightened yet fascinated. Intimate terrorism is happening here on both sides; this is the truth the book tells.

Conveniently, the story that is told in public discussion denies the adult Harrison's seductive agency—however self-destructive. Giving new meaning to the phrase "drama queen" she acts in complicity with a public narrative (not solely of her own making) that makes it seem as though this is a courageous coming-out story where incestuous male violence is being exposed. In some cases Harrison is talked about as though she is now a "*S.C.U.M. Manifesto* radical feminist" warrior in from the trenches. Interviewed by Patricia Towers, Harrison admits that while writing she was tempted "not to take responsibility, to say I may have been twenty, but, in truth, I was a child, and I was taken advantage of. And if I was not physically, brutally forced, then on an emotional level I was forced." Towers affirms this logic by saying, "Which by the way, I think is true." The text succumbs to this temptation. Stylistically, since Harrison skillfully mixes girlhood memories with adult memories and the voice is consistent, readers at times cannot distinguish the two. At times I had to read passages again to see if the experiences described were those of the girl or the woman. Harrison also acknowledges that her other temptation was to characterize herself as "some sort of iconoclast . . . a bad girl . . . a transgressor." While she claims to have sought a middle ground in the text, acknowledging that she "was taken advantage of" and yet "did have responsibility," there is no passage one can cite that even hints at an acknowledgment of responsibility. There is no critical reflection on her choices. Simply writing positive descriptions of the erotic interaction with her father does not convey the agency she implies. Clearly, there are ways in which Harrison wants to be both victim and victor.

Ironically, there are no descriptions of sexual intercourse with either father or other male partners in *The Kiss*. Indeed, Harrison claims not to remember what she actually did sexually with the father. Again this becomes a way to lay claim to the common memory loss incest victims often suffer, but then if we are to believe the Harrison of interviews that she chose this, the writer who remembers all manner of details from early childhood, it seems odd that she cannot remember details of this adult sexual experience. Sensationalizing this narrative, Harrison and the press obscure the reality that much of what this book graphically exposes is not about incest.

In actuality much more than a narrative of incest, the book chronicles Harrison's intense vicious rivalry with her mother, of which consensual incest is one of the weapons of betrayal. It's her own version of *Mommie Dearest* in reverse. As a reader who is not from a culture that insists that hating one's parents is essential to the development of self and identity, I was both awed and appalled by the intensity of Harrison's competition with her mother—the extent to which she saw herself as a rival competing both for the affections of her mother's parents and the love of her absent father. When I first left my southern religious rural working-class world to enter Stanford University, one of the big cultural shocks for me was the extent to which the upper-class white students there expressed hatred and contempt for their parents. Coming from a culture where I was not raised to believe I needed to express hatred of my parents, I found the idea of children competing with parents in power struggles shocking. It fascinates me that this feature of privileged class life is often taken as a norm. Many of my white professional women friends from such backgrounds see nothing strange about the hatred Harrison expresses towards her mother. Naomi Wolf's book *Promiscuities* explores the lives of young white girls from privileged class backgrounds. To her this competition is a norm. She contends "each of us nursed an emerging sexual competition with our mothers."

In *The Kiss* the daughter's hatred is portrayed as a response to her mother's narcissism, her lack of maternal care. Yet the mother's class position allows her to be indifferent to her daughter's needs, knowing that other caregivers will meet them. When it comes to issues her mother thinks are important she asserts parental guidance, yet it is never enough to win her daughter's love. One of the truly moving moments in this book is the description of the caring reunion between the adult Kathryn and her dying mother. Significantly, even that event is eroticized by Harrison. Returning for a final moment alone with her mother's dead body, Harrison writes: "I touch her chest, her arms, her neck; I kiss her forehead and her fingertips. . . . I reach under the bottom half of the lid for the catch to unlock but find none. I slip my hand down as far as I can, past her knees, past the hem of her white dress. I want to touch and know all of her, want her feet in my palms."

Indeed, from the text one can assume that were it not for the vicious rivalry between mother and daughter for center stage in this upper-class extended family household, the dangerous liaison between father and daughter might not have occurred. When Harrison's mother senses that an inappropriate relationship is happening between daughter and father, she takes the young adult Kathryn to a therapist. This becomes another terrain for competition. Kathryn is thrilled that she is able to "win" over her mother by convincing the therapist that nothing is taking place. Before they go to the appointment, Kathryn strategically chooses an outfit that she hopes will enable her to better "seduce" the therapist. Preparing for the visit by wearing a dress so short she confesses that "I can't bend over without my underpants showing," she is thrilled to see that the doctor falls for her and her lies. Her mother tells the psychiatrist, "I think they're having sex." Harrison recalls, "The doctor turns to me, his eyebrows raised, and I lie as I have never lied before or since. I'm a bad liar generally, but on this afternoon, wearing what I'm wearing, I am brilliant. . . . The doctor looks at me sitting before him in my vulgar dress, and he believes me. I know it, and so does my mother. He's mine, not hers, and so I have what I wanted— what I thought I wanted. She is alone. I've taken her husband and now her only ally; the one person with whom she can share her troubles." That Harrison continues to allow her own behavior to be overdetermined by hatred and competition with her mother even after she has left home and entered her own adult life is one of the saddest stories in this book. The fact that she ends the relationship with her father when the mother dies confirms that this competitive bond fueled Harrison's destructive behavior.

According to Harrison, she kept nude photographs her father had taken of her, love letters he had written. Anyone who has studied the literature of coercive incest knows that this is not a common behavior pattern of abuse survivors. Harrison's own pathological narcissism comes through her text as much as her father's fetishization of his "beautiful" daughter. This psychological condition makes her a ripe candidate for the father's seduction, for she is as taken with her own beauty as he is. Significantly, much has been made of Harrison's blond beauty in commentary about the book. In his confessional essay "Sins of the Father," her husband, Colin Harrison, boldly extols her beauty, commenting on the incest by sharing that even though he has fantasized her father's death he can declare: ". . . as another man I dare say I understand a portion of his obsession. There was to be no denying him. There was no denying me." Embedded in this comment are all the old patriarchal ways of justifying male sexual coercion and violence.

In *The Kiss* Harrison's obsession with her blond beauty is always expressed in contrast to her mother's darkness. Throughout the book racial metaphors of darkness and lightness are used to emphasize her specialness. Coming from a family of immigrant Jews whom she describes as dark, she is the golden beauty allied with the Christian father the family has cast out. Harrison comments: "The earliest directive either I or my mother received from her Jewish parents was to form ourselves in opposition to the children around us. Born in London, my grandmother and grandfather have lived all over the world. They've always considered America a land of convenience, hygiene, and safety, and one in which children are 'dragged' as opposed to 'brought' up." Her mother's choice of a Christian with German immigrant ancestors is her way to show contempt towards this Jewish world. Even though Kathryn is a grown woman when she first meets her dad she writes: "The girl my father sees has blond hair that falls past her waist, past her hips; it falls to the point at which her fingertips would brush her thighs if her arms were not crossed before her chest." No reviewers talked about the way in which ethnic and racial tropes formed the symbolic tightrope of the sadomasochistic bond between mother and daughter. The extent to which articles on the book focus on Harrison's "blond beauty" contrasted with the dark world of her upbringing reveal the grave extent to which these tropes, as well as the antisemitism/racism they perpetuate, resonate in contemporary culture. They are so accepted a norm as to be unworthy of comment. A variety of needs are met in this public replaying of the original narrative of dark versus light, sensual educated rich Europe violently coupled with primitive puritanical America, Jew against Christian; the narcissism Christopher Lasch defined as the core of contemporary culture is affirmed, its pathological dimensions rendered normal. The grown-up Harrison can finally have the ongoing intense "gaze" from the parental authority she has longed for, a gaze that bows down to her beauty—to the power of her femininity, a power so intense it conquers all. And the greatest triumph is that Harrison, like the character in the movie *Pretty Woman*, not only transcends the pain of her past, she is rewarded with fame and money. Given such payoffs, "doing it for daddy" appears glamorous. Surely, the marketing of this book personifies the ethos of hedonistic consumerist capitalist patriarchal culture.

While I found *The Kiss* a compelling memoir, it is not exceptionally well written or in any way sensational. Market forces created the sensational atmosphere surrounding publication of the book. Both Harrison and her husband acted in complicity with those forces. Harrison, like the wounded child in her book, seems to glory in the attention she receives, whether positive or negative. Her passion for press suggests that the pathological narcissism so eloquently evoked in the memoir continues to inform her life-choices. Harrison's choices aside, critics clearly chose to critically comment on her writerly persona rather than the content of her text. Were she not a female there would have been no mention made in critical reviews of her longing for fame or her willingness to do whatever it might take to acquire it and she would not have been the target of conservative moral censure. Many male writers are pathologically narcissistic; it is rarely the basis of public critique of their work. Pathological narcissism does not enchant. Tedious and predictable, its presence does not necessarily negate or enhance the power of a writer's work. In Harrison's case it is the vision of herself as a writer that is diminished when she acts in complicity with media's insistence that she justify the content of her memoir.

The work of all women writers is jeopardized when individual female authors are taken to task for the content of their writing. When critiqued on the basis of a double-standard patriarchal morality that led sexist women and men to demand that Harrison justify the content of her book because she is the mother of small children, Harrison simply complied. She did not challenge her critics to examine the sexist biases informing this type of critique. Her response was to tell the world again and again that she had wrestled with the impact her decision to write this book might have on her children and decided that it was best to tell her story. Significantly, her predecessor Anaïs Nin, who was determined to write about sexuality with the same freedom as any male writer, was never asked to justify her work on the basis of motherhood, even though she had a child. That Harrison was subjected to this type of moral critique was both an expression of antifeminist backlash and sexist notions of family values. When did we last hear critics demanding of any male writer that he consider the impact his work might have on his children's lives?

In an article about Harrison titled "Sex with Daddy: Is Disclosure Always Better than Secrecy?" writer Mary Gordon addressed this issue, declaring: "I want to tell her that in making the decision she has, it is impossible that she will avoid muddiness, perhaps not of a literary but of a personal and familial kind. But what is certain is that if she didn't publish this book, something would have been lost to her as both a writer and a human soul. These are the terrible questions that we open ourselves to when we have children." Reading this passage I pondered whether Gordon included male writers when she chose to use the word "we." More than any reaction to Harrison's book, the most troubling one has been the judgmental moralism about whether or not being a mother meant that she should have published this story. Not once did I read any discussion of the book that critiqued the sexism underlying this question. Whenever any writer writes autobiographical work, ethical and moral issues arise. No one speculated about the moral right of Harrison to disclose information about her father or other family members who may not share her vision or her interpretation of the past.

Critics of Harrison deployed a patriarchal vision of the good mother to critique her work on moral grounds. Can we imagine Gordon posing these questions about a male writer: "Had she chosen her writing over her family. Had she exposed her young son and daughter to a lifetime of taunts about their mother and their grandfather." Harrison lacks a feminist vision of herself as a writer, one that would demand an assertion of artistic freedom to create using any subject. She joins the conservative family-values chorus when she dramatically parades in an uncritical manner her sentimental response: "Writing and my children are the two most important things in the world to me. . . . I need to write to know who I am. But the task of being a 'good enough' mother to my children also gives me great solace." In a world where writers are daily confronting issues of censorship, where antifeminist backlash has become an accepted norm, women, along with our male allies in struggle, should be disturbed by any insistence that we judge our writing by patriarchal notions of the good and bad mother.

Whenever a writer of any gender chooses to disclose facts about his or her private life, revealing details about the lives of others without their permission, ethical issues should be considered. The value of ethical concerns about the politics of disclosure are diminished when reduced to the level of whether or not a woman writer's memoir that shares an experience of consensual incest in her life is taking an action that will be harmful to her children. Had Harrison's life choices been more informed by the feminist thinking and feminist movement that was happening in the culture during her twenties her dangerous liaison might never have taken place. Since it did happen and she has chosen to write about it again and again in both her fiction and nonfiction, it is disturbing that she and her critics have not allowed feminist concerns to shape their responses to the work.

Given the power of censorship and antifeminist backlash we should all be insisting that women writers continue to resist silencing. We should uphold and celebrate the rights of women writers to explore our imaginations to the fullest. This freedom can coexist with meaningful critical discussion of the politics of confession and disclosure. While the sensationalist hype and hysteria surrounding Harrison's publication of her memoir will soon pass away, what will remain is the impact critical reception of this work has had on readers and writers. Public reception of this work has been used to serve notice on all women writers that critics will exercise the power to publicly judge and morally condemn the subject of women's writing when it transgresses the boundaries of conservative convention and mainstream decorum. Significantly, writers and readers who value artistic freedom should critically respond—resisting this trend as it diminishes and devalues artistic integrity.

writing autobiography

To me, telling the story of my growing-up years was intimately connected with the longing to kill the self I was without really having to die. I wanted to kill that self in writing. Once that self was gone—out of my life forever—I could more easily become the me of me. It was clearly the Gloria Jean of my tormented and anguished childhood that I wanted to be rid of, the girl who was always wrong, always punished, always subjected to some humiliation or other, always crying, the girl who was to end up in a mental institution because she could not be anything but crazy, or so they told her. She was the girl who sat a hot iron on her arm pleading with them to leave her alone, the girl who wore her scar as a brand marking her madness. Even now I can hear the voices of my sisters saying, "mama make Gloria stop crying." By writing the autobiography, it was not just this Gloria I would be rid of, but the past that had a hold on me, that kept me from the present. I wanted not to forget the past but to break its hold. This death in writing was to be liberatory.

Until I began to try and write an autobiography, I thought that it would be a simple task, this telling of one's story. And yet I tried year after year, never writing more than a few pages. My inability to write out the story I interpreted as an indication that I was not ready to let go of the past, that I was not ready to be fully in the present. Psychologically, I considered the possibility that I had become attached to the wounds and sorrows of my childhood, that I held to them in a manner that blocked my efforts to be self-realized, whole, to be healed. A key message in Toni Cade Bambara's novel *The Salt Eaters*, which tells the story of Velma's suicide attempt, her breakdown, is expressed when the healer asks her, "Are you sure sweetheart, that you want to be well?"

There was very clearly something blocking my ability to tell my story. Perhaps it was remembered scoldings and punishments when mama heard me saying something to a friend or stranger that she did not think should be said. Secrecy and silence—these were central issues. Secrecy about family, about what went on in the domestic household was a bond between us—was part of what made us family. There was a dread one felt about breaking that bond. And yet I could not grow inside the atmosphere of secrecy that had pervaded our lives and the lives of other families about us. Strange that I had always challenged the secrecy, always let something slip that should not be known growing up, yet as a writer staring into the solitary space of paper, I was bound, trapped in the fear that a bond is lost or broken in the telling. I did not want to be the traitor, the teller of family secrets—and yet I wanted to be a writer. Surely, I told myself, I could write a purely imaginative work—a work that would not hint at personal private realities. And so I tried. But always there were the intruding traces, those elements of real life however disguised. Claiming the freedom to grow as an imaginative writer was connected for me with having the courage to be

81

open, to be able to tell the truth of one's life as I had experienced it in writing. To talk about one's life—that I could do. To write about it, to leave a trace—that was frightening.

The longer it took me to begin the process of writing autobiography, the further removed from those memories I was becoming. Each year, a memory seemed less and less clear. I wanted not to lose the vividness, the recall and felt an urgent need to begin the work and complete it. Yet I could not begin even though I had begun to confront some of the reasons I was blocked, as I am blocked just now in writing this piece because I am afraid to express in writing the experience that served as a catalyst for that block to move.

I had met a young black man. We were having an affair. It is important that he was black. He was in some mysterious way a link to this past that I had been struggling to grapple with, to name in writing. With him I remembered incidents, moments of the past that I had completely suppressed. It was as though there was something about the passion of contact that was hypnotic, that enabled me to drop barriers and thus enter fully, rather reenter those past experiences. A key aspect seemed to be the way he smelled, the combined odors of cigarettes, occasionally alcohol, and his body smells. I thought often of the phrase "scent of memory," for it was those smells that carried me back. And there were specific occasions when it was very evident that the experience of being in his company was the catalyst for this remembering.

Two specific incidents come to mind. One day in the middle of the afternoon we met at his place. We were drinking cognac and dancing to music from the radio. He was smoking cigarettes (not only do I not smoke, but I usually make an effort to avoid smoke). As we held each other dancing those mingled odors of alcohol, sweat, and cigarettes led me to say, quite without thinking about it, "Uncle Pete." It was not that I had forgotten Uncle Pete. It was more that I had forgotten the childhood experience of meeting him. He drank often, smoked cigarettes, and always on the few occasions that we met him, he held us children in tight embraces. It was the memory of those embraces—of the way I hated and longed to resist them—that I recalled.

Another day we went to a favorite park to feed ducks and parked the car in front of tall bushes. As we were sitting there, we suddenly heard the sound of an oncoming train—a sound that startled me so that it evoked another long-suppressed memory: that of crossing the train tracks in my father's car. I recalled an incident where the car stopped on the tracks and my father left us sitting there while he raised the hood of the car and worked to repair it. This is an incident that I am not certain actually happened. As a child, I had been terrified of just such an incident occurring, perhaps so terrified that it played itself out in my mind as though it had happened. These are just two ways this encounter acted as a catalyst, breaking down barriers, enabling me to finally write this long-desired autobiography of my childhood.

Each day I sat at the typewriter and different memories were written about in short vignettes. They came in a rush, as though they were a sudden thunderstorm. They came in a surreal, dreamlike style that made me cease to think of them as strictly autobiographical because it seemed that myth, dream, and reality had merged. There were many incidents that I would talk about with my siblings to see if they recalled them. Often we remembered together a general outline of an incident but the details were different for us. This fact was a constant reminder of the limitations of autobiography, of the extent to which autobiography is a very personal storytelling—a unique recounting of events not so much as they have happened but as we remember and invent them. One memory that I would have sworn was "the truth and nothing but

83

the truth" concerned a wagon that my brother and I shared as children. I remembered that we played with this toy only at my grandfather's house, that we shared it, that I would ride it and my brother would push me. Yet one facet of the memory was puzzling—I remembered always returning home with bruises or scratches from this toy. When I called my mother, she said there had never been any wagon, that we had shared a red wheelbarrow, that it had always been at my grandfather's house because there were sidewalks on that part of town. We lived in the hills where there were no sidewalks. Again I was compelled to face the fiction that is a part of all retelling, remembering. I began to think of the work I was doing as both fiction and autobiography. It seemed to fall in the category of writing that Audre Lorde, in her autobiographically based work *Zami*, calls bio-mythography. As I wrote, I felt that I was not as concerned with accuracy of detail as I was with evoking in writing the state of mind, the spirit of a particular moment.

The longing to tell one's story and the process of telling is symbolically a gesture of longing to recover the past in such a way that one experiences both a sense of reunion and a sense of release. It was the longing for release that compelled the writing but concurrently it was the joy of reunion that enabled me to see that the act of writing one's autobiography is a way to find again that aspect of self and experience that may no longer be an actual part of one's life but is a living memory shaping and informing the present. Autobiographical writing was a way for me to evoke the particular experience of growing up southern and black in segregated communities. It was a way to recapture the richness of southern black culture. The need to remember and hold to the legacy of that experience and what it taught me has been all the more important since I have since lived in predominately white communities and taught at predominately white colleges. Black southern folk experience was the foundation of the life around me when I was a child; that experience no longer exists in many places where it was once all of life that we knew. Capitalism, upward mobility, assimilation of other values have all led to rapid disintegration of black folk experience or in some cases the gradual wearing away of that experience.

Within the world of my childhood, we held on to the legacy of a distinct black culture by listening to the elders tell their stories. Autobiography was experienced most actively in the art of telling one's story. I can recall sitting at Baba's (my grandmother on my mother's side) at 1200 Broad Street—listening to people come and recount their life experience. In those days, whenever I brought a playmate to my grandmother's house, Baba would want a brief outline of their autobiography before we would begin playing. She wanted not only to know who their people were but what their values were. It was sometimes an awesome and terrifying experience to stand answering these questions or witness another playmate being subjected to the process and yet this was the way we would come to know our own and one another's family histories. It is the absence of such a tradition in my adult life that makes the written narrative of my girlhood all the more important. As the years pass and these glorious memories grow much more vague, there will remain the clarity contained within the written words.

Conceptually, the autobiography was framed in the manner of a hope chest. I remembered my mother's hope chest, with its wonderful odor of cedar, and thought about her taking the most precious items and placing them there for safekeeping. Certain memories were for me a similar treasure. I wanted to place them somewhere for safekeeping. An autobiographical narrative seemed an appropriate place. Each particular incident, encounter, experience had its own story, sometimes told from the first person, sometimes told from the third person. Often I felt as though I was in a trance at my typewriter, that the shape of a particular memory was decided not by my conscious mind but by all that is dark and deep within me, unconscious but present. It was the act of making it present, bringing it into the open, so to speak, that was liberating.

From the perspective of trying to understand my psyche, it was also interesting to read the narrative in its entirety after I had completed the work. It had not occurred to me that bringing one's past, one's memories together in a complete narrative would allow one to view them from a different perspective, not as singular isolated events but as part of a continuum. Reading the completed manuscript, I felt as though I had an overview not so much of my childhood but of those experiences that were deeply imprinted in my consciousness. Significantly, that which was absent, left out, not included also was important. I was shocked to find at the end of my narrative that there were few incidents I recalled that involved my five sisters. Most of the incidents with siblings were with me and my brother. There was a sense of alienation from my sisters present in childhood, a sense of estrangement. This was reflected in the narrative. Another aspect of the completed manuscript that is interesting to me is the way in which the incidents describing adult men suggest that I feared them intensely, with the exception of my grandfather and a few old men. Writing the autobiographical narrative enabled me to look at my past from a different perspective and to use this knowledge as a means of self-growth and change in a practical way.

In the end I did not feel as though I had killed the Gloria of my childhood. Instead I had rescued her. She was no longer the enemy within, the little girl who had to be annihilated for the woman to

86

come into being. In writing about her, I reclaimed that part of myself I had long ago rejected, left uncared for, just as she had often felt alone and uncared for as a child. Remembering was part of a cycle of reunion, a joining of fragments, "the bits and pieces of my heart" that the narrative made whole again.

from public to private

writing *bone black*

When I first told everybody around me that I was writing a memoir, the initial response was usually "Aren't you rather young to be doing that?" A great many people still think that memoirs should be written late in life, in a moment of reflection and response when one is old and retired. Such thinking seems oddly old-fashioned given that we are living at a time when it is clearly evident that a great many of us will never live to a ripe old age. As never in my life before the young are dying around me or preparing for the possibility of early death. And like many folks in their mid-forties I am stunned by the number of friends, comrades, and/or peers who have passed away just when life was becoming most sweet. Among this mounting dead are well-known writers and artists who leave few if any autobiographical traces. Already there is an aura of unreconcilable loss that is assuredly a response to knowing that we will never hear them tell their stories.

Frankly, I begin to write *Bone Black*, the memoir of my girlhood, almost twenty years ago. In my late twenties still grappling psychoanalytically with emotional disturbances that were directly related to childhood I turned to autobiography to have a more condensed yet complete picture. I wrote about significant memories, the little incidents and stories I had heard myself tell again and again to explain something about myself. These memories flowed from me in a lyrical poetic prose that fascinated me. My usual writing style was clear and direct. These mysterious, dreamlike visions of the past appeared in an uncalculated manner. The style intrigued me; I felt it was the closest I had ever come to divinely inspired writing.

When I first began writing *Bone Black: Memories of Girlhood* I did not have a plan. My assumption was just that I would write the story of my life and that it would unfold on the page in a conventional documentary fashion. Yet when I began to write, having made no conscious decisions about style or content, the writing that emerged was not the conventional autobiographical format. The style was lyrical, poetic, and abstract. It was not the straightforward linear narrative that characterized my previous nonfiction work. The writing was different from anything I had imagined, but I liked it. For what appeared on the page were words that evoked the spirit of the world I grew up in and that spirit unfolding in its own manner and fashion moved me. A gentle, tender intimacy was evoked in the words, I felt it. I felt the reader would feel it as well, and so I let the style of the work inspire and claim me.

Any writer who strives to be true to artistic integrity surrenders to the shape the work takes of its own accord. Work comes to a writer differently depending on our circumstances at the time of writing. The politics of experience and location shape our vision. My first book, *Ain't I a Woman: Black Women and Feminism,* was written shortly after I left the racial apartheid of my growing up. As a black female coming from a southern, working-class, fundamentalist Christian background, it was incredibly difficult for me to speak with a radical voice, to let go my fear and find the right words. Initially, I wanted to address and appease so many different audiences that the book in its early stages was this wordy, overly pedantic work—full of the academic styles I had learned were appropriate in my undergraduate English classes. I rewrote this book again and again until I found my style, a voice that sounded real to me and not a mere imitation of the fake academic neutral sound I had learned to cultivate in academic settings. The first version of this work was finished when I was nineteen but the book was not published until years later. By then my style was distinct and clear. I worked on refining it for future works. So it was a tremendous surprise to me when *Bone Black* developed in a direction that was more akin to the style I had as a poet.

Admittedly, I began writing *Bone Black* as part of a psychoanalytic effort to understand the past. When I sent proposals of the work with sample chapters to publishers, I was told again and again that the work was not interesting in its lyrical poetic prose style but if I would just "tell the story," i.e., convert it all to linear narratives, it would be acceptable. While we like to imagine ours is not a publishing world that promotes and encourages censorship, it became clear to me that there was a style of African-American writing, particularly work by women, that was acceptable; anything outside the mold was ignored or rejected.

When I began this work more than ten years ago memoirs were not as compelling to readers as they are today. When I sent samples of this work to editors they were not the slightest bit interested. Editors seemed to think the story of my girlhood would be more compelling in the marketplace if it was sensational. They wanted me to tell my story in the good old-fashioned manner of tabloid-like confession or straightforward autobiography. I wanted to tell this story on its own terms, respecting the integrity of artistic vision. Recently, there has been a shift in literary attitudes concerning confessional writing. Memoirs are now regarded more highly. Currently, they have value because there have been many stories that were best-sellers. Of course memoirs that make the most money are most often those that have sensational appeal. Yet this fact of the current marketplace does not make the memoir an inferior or less than literary genre. As a reader who enjoys well-crafted autobiographical writing, I have been thrilled by new and stylistically innovative memoirs. I was excited by the more recent celebration of the memoir. It made it possible for me to return to my earlier memoir writing and complete it.

In the preface to *Bone Black: Memories of Girlhood* I stated my reasons for writing and publishing this book at this time, calling attention to the growing body of psychological and sociological feminist writings on girlhood and the paucity of information about black girlhood. I emphasized the fact that when black girlhood is talked about novels are the text evoked. Without in any way diminishing the importance of novels about black girlhood, I stressed that fiction cannot be used by critical thinkers as a base for accurate ethnographic comprehension of this experience, that nonfiction accounts are needed. Documenting my own experience was an act of critical intervention. A growing body of fictional accounts of girlhood exist that graphically tell narratives of rape, incest, and overall abuse in black girlhood. These accounts are often drawn from true stories and embellished. *Bone Black* tells the story of my attempt to construct self and identity in a troubled home environment. Most specifically it paints a portrait of an artistic, gifted child in a working-class southern religious household whose yearning to read, think, and write are at odds with family expectations. There is much psychological conflict, torture, and physical pain, which when I was an adolescent led me to feel suicidal. The girlhood decision of whether or not I should kill myself is consistently juxtaposed with the struggle to find my place as thinker, dreamer, and emerging writer. In many ways it is a common story of adolescent alienation—an account of the feelings of a misunderstood outsider who cannot find a place to belong.

Much to my surprise none of the reviews I read mentioned suicide. This was the case even when reviews overwhelmingly praised the work. Indeed, a number of reviews (largely by white women), though written with positive intent, implied that though full of "marvelous" lyrical prose there was nothing really significant happening in the book—no story. Black woman writer Thulani Davis took the book to task for its lack of graphic revelation. Based on her understanding of my previous work she concludes, "One might expect a memoir of utter clarity, rendered without sentiment." She concludes her piece with the statement that these "memories of girlhood may seem no more than moments safely told of the ordinary days of an extraordinary person." Since she does not refer to the suicidal longings expressed in the memoir, readers cannot know if she thinks such longings are safe and ordinary. Like many reviewers, Davis seemed unable to let go her desire to hear a particular kind of gutsy down-to-earth account of a gifted black girl growing up in a troubled family long enough to appreciate the significance of my chosen narrative content and style.

There is nothing sensational in *Bone Black*, no rape, no prolonged graphically violent beatings, no incest. It is not a "safe" book, as it resists contempt for the ordinary, reminding readers that we are as marked by small, seemingly trivial moments in life as we are by dramatic incidents. The suicidal longings of an adolescent girl are not the stuff of great intrigue, nor did I want them to be. I wanted to show how one can be terribly isolated and desperate while calmly embracing the mundane. From the onset I was concerned that it would be difficult to interest a reading public so inclined toward the sensational that I was not confident that a more lyrical imaginative account of black female experience could find a place. So many stories of black girlhood are filled with lurid tales of all manner of sexual abuse, incest, rape by strangers, and unrelenting violence that this has almost come to represent in the popular imagination what black girlhood is. To deviate from this "norm," whether by describing similar situations without sensationalism or offering a completely different account, in many readers' minds would be tantamount to a betrayal of conventional stereotypical assumptions about black girlhood. For the most part mainstream reviewers did not know what to make of this book. It simply did not fit their expectations.

While the book was received warily by mainstream reviewers, reviews in the alternative press grappled with the work on its own terms. Usually, black reviewers, with the exception of writer Thulani Davis, directly addressed the content of the book. They were not concerned about my public persona or whether this book "fit" with the other books I had written. Black writers, like all authors from marginal groups, always have difficulty gaining recognition for a body of work if anything we do is eclectic. Positive reception of our early work may mean that we are positioned by the critical and reading public in specific ways. Deviating from this may cause them confusion.

This is especially the case for American-born black writers. Writers born in the Caribbean or Africa who come to literary prominence tend to be given greater leeway to write in diverse styles than African-American writers. A prime example of this would be the work of Jamaica Kincaid, who was born in St. Johns, Antigua, in the West Indies. Kincaid writes fiction, nonfiction, and autobiographical work. When she uses diverse styles it is seen as a sign of her literary prowess. Her most recent work, *My Brother,* clearly fits in the category of memoir, simply defined as a record of events based on the writer's personal observation. Even so, in a rather disingenuous way Kincaid attempted to disassociate her work from the genre, stating: "In fact, the advance copy of the book had the word memoir on it and I made them remove it. When it comes out in hardcover it won't have it. A memoir is too generous and big a word, it's certainly inappropriate for anything that I would write. It's a marketing word that doesn't apply to the work. Writers really should pay attention to these things. How can you call a work a memoir when you're writing about a thing that's ongoing? A memoir is when the thing has stopped, and these events that I've written about, they are still ongoing in my life. I'm not yet at the age to write a memoir." These statements notwithstanding, *My Brother* is a work that contains a writer's observations and reflections on her brother's death; it is a memoir.

There are times in my writing career when I envy the freedom black writers who are not born in the United States have to create work that is not seen through the narrow lens that has traditionally determined the critical scope of readers' responses to writing by African-Americans. Despite commonalities, writing by black writers who are not African-Americans tends to be seen as always more literary and therefore more valuable than work by African-Americans. Even though I have always loved reading, valuing the library as a place to read books free of charge, it was not until I went away to college that I first read a wide range of literature by black writers in the diaspora. Growing up, as I did, in a social situation of racial apartheid where books by African-American writers were usually impossible to find because public libraries in segregated small towns simply did not order them, my big quest was to find these books and read them. I was desperate to find them because if they were not there it would mean that I had little chance of succeeding at becoming a writer.

Many black American writers born before the days of racial integration, especially those of us from poor and working-class backgrounds, relied on caring librarians to aid us in our discovery of the world of books. Indeed, the white librarians were often among the most generous educators when it came to working with black students. While other teachers imposed their racial biases the librarians usually urged us to read. And those of us who cared about books were given guidance. It was the white librarian at the public library whom I dared tell in my girlhood that I wanted to read books by black writers. While she did not know about them, she was willing to search for them and show me how to find them.

In those days, I did not think about the fate of black writers in the diaspora. My sense of the literary universe had been shaped by the canon of great writing by white westerners. From the moment I entered college I sought to expand my reading horizons. When preparing for my doctorate I chose as one of my areas of concentration African literature, both francophone and anglophone. I read black writers of the diaspora, focusing my attention on writers from Africa and the Caribbean. When reading experimental work by Guyanese writer Wilson Harris or the work of South African writer Bessie Head, I often discussed with classmates the different impact colonization and white supremacy had on those writers and their visions and those of African-American writers. It seemed to me then and now that more of them felt free to articulate their vision in diverse styles than African-American writers. This is especially the case with the work that is in any way experimental.

All too often it is assumed (especially by white critics) that the black writer who is not African-American is inherently more serious and literary. While a writer like Jamaica Kincaid is often asked in interviews to offer her pronouncements and judgments about black American writing and culture, African-Americans doing work that is serious literature are not asked to give our views on the nature of Caribbean or African writing and culture. Unfortunately, more often than not known black writers who are not African-American seek to distance themselves from the forms of censorship in the publishing world that check, control, and shape African-American writing. Taking advantage of the racist stereotypes that inform literary biases, these writers often accept without question and perpetuate the stereotypical notions about black American writing that continue to abound in our culture.

All too often one of those stereotypes is that the African-American with token exceptions is not interested in the craft of writing. Hence even if we use experimental styles or write using diverse stylistic strategies we will be judged by a conventional yardstick that demands that we always and only speak from our gut, tell our stories using only one literary paradigm. Writing and publishing *Bone Black* reinforced both my awareness of the ways in which African-American writing, especially the work of black women writers, gets pigeonholed by both the publishing industry and the reading public. When we experiment with diverse styles, when the content and shape of our work goes against the stereotypical grain we risk it being devalued by a critical reviewing public that does not know how to approach the work. Challenging biases in the reviewing process as well as demanding of publishers that they remain open when selecting work by African-Americans so that unconventional material is not discarded or rewritten to appeal to the marketplace is necessary if we are to gain greater freedom to write what we want to write in the manner in which we wish to write it.

class and the politics
of writing

No one speaks about class and the politics of writing in this society. It is just assumed that everyone has equal opportunity when it comes to writing and publishing. Taken seriously such an assumption seems ludicrous, given the reality that so many citizens of our nation do not read or write and that most of what is published comes from an educated elite who are either from privileged class backgrounds or are aspiring to enter privileged classes. On panels when I have even dared to mention that there may be a relation between what we write, what we feel we are allowed to say, and our class background, audiences have vehemently disagreed. This is especially the case when the topic is confessional writing. When I have suggested that groups of people who come from class backgrounds where there are rituals of public confession like psychoanalysis are socialized to be more accepting of self-disclosure in public, audiences respond by trying to negate this thesis, arguing that everyone has these issues. I concur that everyone confronts the issues but maintain that class background often overdetermines the nature of that response.

Women of color from poor and working-class backgrounds have been among those writers who have most called attention to grappling with the question of authorial freedom as it relates to autobiographical revelation in published work. Many of us live with the fear that if we write about certain experiences, individuals we have written about, particularly family members, will punish that writing through ostracization. When I was a student in writing classes and at writing workshops I never really heard anyone from a privileged class background talk about self-censorship that emerges from fear that writing certain experiences will lead family and friends to break ties. In some cases writers from privileged classes were much more likely to hold a vision of writerly integrity that implied for them that there should be no discussion of the ethics of revealing aspects of another person's life who has not given their consent. From the moment I began to talk about the lives of members of my family, including their stories in my work, I began to think about the ethics of such writing.

When contemporary feminist movement raised the question of women's silences, of taboos about what women could talk and write about, individual women of color were among that group who shared their fear of coming to voice, of speaking the unspeakable. In the third book I published, *Talking Back,* I concluded the introductory essay with these remarks: "While punishing me, my parents often spoke about the necessity of breaking my spirit. Now when I ponder the silences, the voices that are not heard, the voices of those wounded and/or oppressed individuals who do not speak or write, I contemplate the acts of persecution, torture—the terrorism that breaks spirits, that makes creativity impossible. I write these words to bear witness to the primacy of resistance struggle in any situation of domination (even within family life); to the strength and power that emerges from sustained resistance and the profound conviction that these forces can be healing, can protect us from dehumanization and despair." Before many of us even confronted the issue of confessional writing we had to grapple with the more basic question of claiming writing as a site for the articulation of our realities, especially nonfiction writing. Acknowledging this struggle in her work *The Last Generation*, Cherrie Moraga declares: "Fundamentally, I started writing to save my life. Yes, my own life first. I see the same impulse in my students—the dark, the queer, the mixed-blood, the violated—turning to the written page with a relentless passion, a drive to avenge their own silence, invisibility, and erasure as living, innately expressive human beings." Again, the new ground that we were breaking at the onset of contemporary feminist movement concerns writing that is explicitly autobiographical and confessional. Moraga contends: "A writer will write with or without a movement; but at the same time, for Chicano, lesbian, gay, and feminist writers—anybody writing against the grain of Anglo misogynist culture—political movements are what have allowed our writing to surface from the secret places in our notebooks into the public sphere." After struggling to come to voice we then confronted ethical issues.

Since many of us were young writers (I was nineteen years old when I completed the first version of *Ain't I a Woman: Black Women and Feminism*) we were trying to figure out how to find publishers. Even though we saw our writing as a form of resistance we were not clear about the way the mainstream publishing world would respond to that writing. Early on mainstream publishing just rejected most of this work, which is why so many of us looked to alternative publishing. In those days we did not talk a great deal about the consequences of writing openly about one's life because most of us had not reached that level. In my first books, I did not emphasize the personal. I shared very little about my life. This was a reflection of both the academic training I had received as a graduate student of English and my own fear of the personal. I was not eager to talk about my life precisely because I had been raised in a working-class southern black Christian home where talking openly outside the family about any aspect of family life was considered a form of treason. Similarly describing her experience in a poor white southern household Dorothy Allison shares: "I had been taught never to tell anyone outside my family what was going on, not just because it was so shameful but because it was physically dangerous for me to do so. . . . I didn't start writing—or rather I didn't start keeping my writing—until 1974, when I published a poem. Everything I wrote before then, ten years of journals and short stories and poems, I burned, because I was afraid somebody would read them." Some of us feared violent responses from family members. This was true of Asian and Chicana women writers I knew as well. While many of us wrote of the power and passion of coming to voice it was rare that anyone shared publicly the response to their work on the part of intimate family and friends.

I began to write about my life as a way of reaching out to readers across class and race. Since I was writing feminist theory I saw it as a necessary political dimension of that work to strive to make it as accessible as possible. Initially, I shared my work with my family and bore the brunt of harsh criticism from my mother. She was especially disappointed when I began to describe our family as dysfunctional in print. My writing was an act of resistance not simply in relation to outer structures of domination like race, sex, and class; I was writing to resist all the socialization I had received in a religious, southern, working-class, patriarchal home that tried to teach me silence as the most desirable trait of womanliness. Writing about the ways I was often punished, particularly for the offense of talking back, I shared in published work both the pain and isolation I felt as a girl dreaming about ideas and writing as well as the punishment I received for refusing to be silent.

My mother felt particularly targeted by my work; she felt I was publicly blaming her. Even though I tried to explain again and again the way writers draw on their own lives fully acknowledging that my interpretation of the past would differ from hers, she felt and continues to feel hurt by my autobiographical work. Any description of someone in the family that does not resemble her memory is perceived as false. Neither of my parents attended college. They have not had the experience of writing about their lives, or even speaking much about their lives in any unfamiliar setting. Even though writers from privileged class backgrounds may write work that alienates family members, there is a much greater chance that shared educational backgrounds will enable them to understand the process of writing even if they do not agree with what is written. At times I fear my parents will read something I have written about our family and excommunicate me forever. When I sit down to write I ward off that part of me that would censor my words to protect our silences, that would keep intact the intimacy of our secrets.

This fear of being cut off by family members for writing stuff they may not understand, whether it be autobiographical or nonfiction, surfaces in all the writers I have known from working-class backgrounds no matter their race or region of origin. In the essay "Telling Stories of Queer White Trash," Jillian Sandell contends: "In a culture that promotes storytelling and the confessional narrative to almost hyperbolic proportions, the fact that stories about impoverished whites have been virtually untellable suggests a profound collective anxiety about what such narratives might reveal."

When I first met Dorothy Allison, a writer who like myself was writing about rural southern experience, about poverty, in her case being seen as "white trash," and neglect, abuse, and abandonment, weaving together narratives about race, sex, and class, and in her case lesbian identity, we had more in common than I have had with most straight black writers from privileged class backgrounds, who had no understanding of what it means to write "against the grain." Dorothy Allison has shared with many of us both in conversations and in her recent essays how writing about family members has affected their lives. Early on in her work, by merging her autobiographical and fictional narratives, she was able to "protect" family members even as she disclosed much about her life, simply because the reader did not know what was true and what was fiction. Still, her family knew and even though they did not always remember as she did they tried to understand.

In her collection of essays *Skin: Talking About Sex, Class and Literature* Allison talks about the difficulty of writing from an autobiographical place even if the work you do is mainly fiction. She writes about her worries that being open about sexuality from a lesbian perspective might "endanger" her relationship to her son by providing information that could be perversely used to take him away from her. Yet when she enters the writing process she gives herself over fully without allowing her words to be shaped by fear of censure: "When I am writing I sink down into myself, my memory, dreams, shames, and terrors. I answer questions no one has asked but me, avoid issues no one else has raised, and puzzle out just where my responsibility begins and ends." Not all writers from poor and working-class backgrounds grapple with ethical issues. Some folks simply turn their backs on the past, writing into a world of class privilege where it is better if they let the past go. Those of us who struggle to maintain our allegiance to the class of our family of origin are continually faced with issues of accountability and responsibility. Whereas folks with money who are written about in ways that they do not like can sue or even challenge family members in print, our relatives have no spaces to "talk back." Often we write about their responses to our work to give them presence beyond our interpretive representations. In Allison's essay "Skin, Where She Touches Me" she reveals: "Some of what I wrote had been painful for my mama to read, but she had never suggested I should not write those stories and publish them. 'I've never been afraid of the truth,' she told me after my book of short stories came out." How fortunate Allison is to receive such a response. Many writers from working-class backgrounds have not been as fortunate.

The responses of family to my work vary. Not surprisingly, among my seven siblings those who have attended college and taken courses in writing are more supportive. Since I often draw on the lives of my six sisters and my brother Kenneth, if I am saying anything about them that might be in the slightest bit harmful I talk about it with them first, of course hoping that they will affirm the writing. This was especially crucial when I began to make references to my sister Valeria's lesbianism. Before publishing any work that identified her, I needed her permission. Just as it has not been a simple manner for me to write publicly about our private family life, I do not believe it was a simple choice for her to affirm and encourage what I chose about her reality, especially as neither of us can control the manner in which this information is received. Of all my siblings, Valeria is the most understanding about the process of writing. Even when she does not agree with my interpretations of our family reality, she supports my freedom to tell my story as I perceive. Neither of us believes there is any absolute "true" account of one's life, since when talking together about the past we may remember the same experience in radically different ways. In one of my books I shared an incident that involved one of my married sisters and her family. While I mentioned to her that I was telling this story, neither of us saw any need to ask permission of her husband. And even though he was not a usual reader of my work, somehow he found this passage and it caused conflict. Again, I am describing situations faced by individuals from poor and working-class backgrounds who have never had to think about whether a relative would write something about their lives.

As my writing became increasingly autobiographical I felt even more fear that my parents might stop speaking to me because of their disapproval of what I say. After a particularly bitter disagreement with my mother about my public sharing of an experience that disclosed information about the family, I wrote them a letter to explain my writing process. In the opening paragraph I stated: "I am writing you both to say that I am sorry that my public sharing of experiences that have deeply affected me hurts you. It is not my intention or desire to cause you pain. And if my actions are hurting please be forgiving. All my life I have worked to be an open honest person who has nothing to hide, who does not feel shame about anything that has happened in my life. And while I have chosen to talk about painful memories in my work, I also speak about joyful memories. There is nothing about the pain of the past that I have not forgiven, but forgiveness does not mean that one forgets. It is my deep belief than in talking about the past, in understanding the things that have happened to us we can heal and go forward." Throughout the letter I expressed my gratitude to my parents for doing the best job of raising us that they could do given the circumstances, sharing the ways I feel appreciation can coexist with critical awareness.

Initially, I had wanted to tell them that writers always draw on their lives but I realized this would have been dishonest. Not all writers draw on their lives. And certainly most black women do not choose to reveal intimate details of their personal lives. Instead I wrote: "As a writer who has chosen to do autobiographical writing I realize that I share information publicly that you would not share. My hope is that you will respect my right to tell my story as I see it even though you do not always agree with what is being told or the decision to speak about it publicly." After sending this letter I waited to see if there would be any discussion. My parents never said a word. Even when I asked them if they had received it they said nothing. I had no way to know if my efforts at explanation had made anything clearer. What I live with is the reality that writing about my life has created an emotional distance between me and my parents. An intimacy we once shared is gone.

Oftentimes I have heard black women writers suggest that they will share certain aspects of their lives when their parents are no longer living. Their confidence that they will outlive their parents surprises me. In part, the awareness that so many black women writers die young has compelled me to write openly and honestly about aspects of my life I would have once believed would be best shared in old age. Such a long list exists of black women writers who have not made it to old age. There is so much about the writing life of Zora Neale Hurston, Lorraine Hansberry, Pat Parker, Audre Lorde, Toni Cade Bambara that we will never know. They did not live long enough to become old.

So much of what is written about the lives of working-class people in our culture, whether in fiction or nonfiction, comes to us from the perspective of those who either have not known such lives or imagine them only through a bourgeois perspective. As I moved into a realm of class privilege, further and further away from the working-class world of my origin, just as I began to see a shift in my language (more and more I was losing my southern accent—that long slow Kentucky drawl as if we are beating words with a broom) I could also see a shift in the nature of memories, so I began to write them. Long before I published my first memoir, a narrative of girlhood, I had begun to write those memories. I wanted them on paper before they became the stuff of romantic nostalgia.

Frankly the world in which working-class girls of any race or ethnicity could begin to write in the spaces of their family of origin rarely exists. More than ever before it seems the idea of writing serious literature becomes the terrain of those who are privileged, who have the "right" education. Even though their feelings about my writing are mixed, it was in the heart of my working-class family that I chose to become a writer. My love of books and words was affirmed at times and at other times negated but was never destroyed by relentless assault. There are many other girls and boys from working-class backgrounds who had to hide their books and their words for fear of punishment. Writing about her working-class upbringing in the essay "Art and Life" Jeanette Winterson recalls hiding books under her mattress: "But as my collection grew, I began to worry that my mother might notice that her daughter's bed was rising visibly. One day she did. She burned everything."

My family's response was always much more ambiguous. There were those times when they threatened to take books away and even to burn them. Then there were the times when mama pleaded with daddy and saved to buy a book I longed for. Like many working-class parents, they were afraid that "too much book learning" would make me unfit for my station in life. Even though we lived in a culture that did not talk about class, they lived the reality of class boundaries. They had not shifted from the poor and working-class backgrounds of their families of origin and there was no precedent to strengthen hopes that any of their children would enter the ranks of the middle class. Their hope was that we would work hard in our jobs, create families, lead decent lives.

Often when I am lecturing or reading from my work, individuals from privileged class backgrounds will come up to me wanting to know how I escaped my class of origin. Always, they say to me that my parents must be so proud. My parents are proud. And when they see all my books lined up on a bookstore shelf and when they see the prices readers pay for them they are impressed. Yet their pride is mingled with bitterness and regret. While they are pleased that I have not betrayed my class, become an uppity intellectual and writer who looks down on them and other poor and working-class women and men, they are saddened that family secrets have been told. No doubt they wish for me a different kind of writing, a different kind of success.

While I have no regret, I am saddened that writers from poor and working-class backgrounds must still count the emotional costs should they dare to reveal that which the world would choose to leave unspoken, with no written account. We all know that there are times when counting the costs acts to silence and censor. Writers from working-class backgrounds, women and men of color who have only recently found our way to the printed page (in the last twenty years) who do not choose to leave behind these worlds or make of them fodder for the entertainment of a prurient privileged class are continuously struggling to find ways to bridge gaps and maintain ties. This work is as much a part of the writing process as putting words on paper. The way we do what we do makes a cultural space, a gap in the system, so that there will always be an opening for the poor and working class to find their way to words, to writing, to print, a way that need not be marked by bitterness, betrayal, and regret.

a life in the spirit

faith, writing, and intellectual work

Touched by the mystical dimensions of Christian faith when I was a girl, I felt the presence of the Beloved in my heart, the Oneness of all life. At that time, when I had not acquired knowledge of appropriate terminology, I only knew that despite the troubles of my world, the suffering I witnessed around and within me, there was always a spiritual force that lifted me higher and gave me moments of transcendent bliss wherein I could surrender all thought of the world and know profound peace. Religious ecstasy was real. I knew its rapture. My heart had been touched by its delight. Early on, I made a commitment to be a seeker on the Path, a seeker after Truth. I was determined to live a life in the spirit.

Black religious experience as I knew and lived it growing up was a liberation theology. For generations, black churchgoers had used the gospel to re-vision our understandings of black experience, to make radical sense of our history, and to build communities of resistance that enabled us to protest and struggle for freedom. Long before I had ever read any Marxism, any works on liberation theology from Latin America, I knew that my destiny was inextricably linked to that of the poor. Each week I had the task of reading to the church from those passages in the book of Matthew that declare: "Come ye blessed of my father, inherit the kingdom prepared for you from the foundation of the world. For I was hungry and you gave me meat, I was thirsty and you gave me drink: I was a stranger, and you took me in: Naked, and you clothed me: I was sick, and you visited me: I was in prison and you came to me." When the righteous respond by expressing surprise and wonder as to when they did these things, they were told: "Inasmuch as you have done it unto one of the least of these my brethren, you have done it unto me" (Matthew 25:34–40). In the church of my youth, I learned that our spiritual work was to meet the needs of the poor and the downtrodden. So it was as a young girl attending Virginia Baptist Church in Kentucky that I became politicized. I learned then that it was not enough to identify with the poor; one had to act to transform society and human lives so that we would all have access to paradise. Our mission was to make a beloved community in the world, where everyone would be free to live well.

In my church, I learned to be contemplative yet to know the importance of realizing one's faith in actions, in concrete gestures of community, in service. In *Seeking the Heart of Wisdom*, Jack Kornfield explains the path of service: "For many people service and open-hearted giving become the very vehicles for their liberation and are taken as their path or way of practice. A sense of interconnectedness leads to the realization that all our activity can be undertaken as service to the world around us." An ethic of service was a fundamental aspect of the religious and secular black experience I knew in my childhood and I was taught how to serve. Those teachings were combined with an emphasis on dedication to truth. Reflecting on the way traditional black religious experience emphasizes the need for truth, black theologian James Cone in *God of the Oppressed* asserts: "Indeed our survival and liberation depend upon our recognition of the truth when it is spoken and lived by the people. If we cannot recognize the truth, then it cannot liberate us from untruth. To know the truth is to appropriate it, for it is not mainly reflection and theory. Truth is divine action entering our lives and creating the human action of liberation." My faith was stronger than that of the world around me. In living that faith I learned not only that grown folks did not always express Truth, but that sometimes they stood in the way, blocking the path. Consequently, it was necessary at times to rebel against their authority.

In remembering my youth, I emphasize the mystical dimensions of Christian faith because it was that aspect of religious experience that I found to be truly liberatory. The more fundamental, rigid beliefs that were taught to me, urging blind obedience to authority and acceptance of oppressive hierarchies, did not move me. No, it was those mystical experiences that enabled me to recognize that the Beloved offers us a realm of being and spiritual experience that transcends the law, that is beyond the authority of man. In her essay "The Feminist Mystic," Mary Giles clarifies the way females trained in traditional sexist thinking and behavior were often compelled by spiritual devotion to become disloyal to patriarchy and to men. Writing about Teresa of Avila, Giles comments: "Even though Teresa did not always have guidance in prayer from spiritually wise confessors, she continued to pray, for the light within was strong enough to withstand ignorance without." Ultimately, according to Giles, Teresa felt her rebellion against male authority sanctioned by grace and urged her spiritual sisters to remember "the authority of the heart overrides that of the mind—even when the heart is a woman's and the mind's a man." Growing up was a time of intense contemplation for me. It was during that time of my life that I learned to build an inner life that could sustain me. I felt even then that I was on a spiritual journey. In my church, we often sang the words "Is it well with your soul? Are you free and made whole?" As a seeker on the Path, I was searching for a way to be well in my soul.

Although I considered myself living a life in the spirit, I went away to college knowing that I would no longer participate fully in the organized church, which over the years had come to seem full of folks who really did not believe what they taught or live those beliefs. During my undergraduate years, I began to look at other religious traditions in search of new and different spiritual paths. I was seeking to flee a fundamentalist religious tradition that was firmly rooted in the notion of punishment. I could no longer accept Western metaphysical dualism: the assumption that the world was divided into good and bad, white and black, superior and inferior. In *Original Blessing*, Matthew Fox best expresses the dilemma I felt as a young woman raised in the southern black Baptist tradition when he writes of the pitfalls of a model of spirituality exclusively structured around the drama of fall and redemption:

> It is a dualistic model and a patriarchal one; it begins its theology with sin and original sin, and it generally ends with redemption. Fall/redemption spirituality does not teach believers about the New Creation or creativity, about justice-making and social transformation, or about Eros, play, pleasure and the God of delight. It fails to teach love of the Earth or care for the cosmos, and it is so frightened of passion that it fails to listen to the impassioned pleas of the *anawim*, the little ones of human history. . . .

As a young adult woman able to be critical of Christianity, I searched for a spiritual path that would offer an alternative to the fall/redemption model. That search led me to teachings and to spiritual leaders and guides who taught me about other paths. I learned about the mystical dimensions of Islam, studied about Buddhism, Hinduism, and other religious traditions. My current spiritual practice grows out of a combination of various traditions. Drawn to the teachings of Buddha, I practice yoga and meditation. That aspect of Christian faith I most cling to is the emphasis on prayer. And from the teachings of Sufi mystics, I learned how to understand Love as divine energy in the universe.

During my twenties, as I searched for the "correct" path, one that would speak most intimately to me, I began to think of spiritual practice as a way of being that was private, that I did not need to share with others in words. Striving also to become a self-actualized intellectual, I stayed in college. The academic environments that were the primary sites of my educational experiences placed little value on spiritual life. Indeed, my peers and colleagues mostly thought of religion as a kind of joke. They ridiculed and mocked the idea that any smart person could sustain belief in God. So it may have been that this atmosphere also led me to take my spiritual beliefs inward. I never thought then that the university was overall a place hostile to religious practice, but in retrospect I can see that it was. Interviewed in *The Other Side*, Henri Nouwen, remembering his time at Harvard, reminds us of the way the deeply competitive nature of universities can disrupt spiritual practice. Commenting on his years there, Nouwen shares: "It's not an intimate place. It's a place of intellectual battle. On the one hand, I loved being there—I made some beautiful friends. But at the same time, I didn't feel it was a safe place where I could deepen my spiritual life." During my undergraduate years at Stanford, I would often seek refuge in the church that Leland Stanford built in memory of his son. There in the ornate quietness, I would struggle to remember the Beloved, to be still and know God. In those days, the church was more than just a place for tourists and fancy weddings; one could go there to regain a sense of the sacred. In my graduate years, there was no such place. I learned to look within.

As certain as I was in my youth that I was on a spiritual journey, I worked to live in the spirit even as I also worked to strengthen my knowledge of and involvement in progressive politics. In my undergraduate years, I began to think deeply about feminism. Struggling to be self-actualized, I knew that the experience of being black and female had to be understood as similar to and yet different from white female reality. During those years, I began writing my first book, *Ain't I a Woman: Black Women and Feminism.* The writing of this book was for me a journey that was both spiritual and political. Remembering the teacher and mystic Howard Thurman's love for the concert of journeying (he called one of his books *The Inward Journey*), Luther Smith explains:

> It suggests searching, exploring, having the spirit of adventure to discover meaning. It is an adventure of exposure and risk. It requires one to embrace the unknown as a given of the trip, and perhaps even as one's destination. It will take courage, strength, trust, and discipline to travel successfully; in other words, it is in journey that spiritual character is forged.

Before I wrote *Ain't I a Woman: Black Women and Feminism*, the image of myself that I identified with was that of a bohemian artist concerned first and foremost with art—sometimes that would be painting, at other times writing poetry. I had begun to do both as a child. Thinking of my vision as political, as one that might serve as a guide influencing others, had not occurred to me. When I felt an inward "spiritual" call to explore the social and political implications of black femaleness in relation to the feminist movement, I resisted.

Listening to my heart, I felt called in the direction of the feminist movement, and I was reluctant to answer the call. It was one thing to espouse radical ideas, especially about gender; it was quite another matter to become actively politically engaged. Not yet twenty years old, I was convinced that my faith would always be challenged by whether I could sacrifice ego-centered longings for a more collective good. I answered the call of voices deep within me and began to write a book about black women and feminism. Journeying deeper into a realm of critical thinking and political consciousness that had been initially stirred by the life and work of Malcolm X, I began to find myself more at odds with the world around me. By the time I entered graduate school, I had finished this book and thought I could return to that old identity, focusing once again solely on literature, art, and a world of creative writing. This was not to be. I was not the same person.

When I first published a chapbook of poems, *And There We Wept*, I had chosen to use as a pseudonym my great-grandmother's name, Bell Hooks. Though there were many reasons for choosing and keeping a pen name, the one I seldom talked about was my religious belief that it was important to deflect away from self and ego. Using another name was for me a spiritual exercise. It meant that I had to give up a particular kind of recognition that comes when our person is more directly identified with the work that we do. Another aspect of this exercise was that the pen name was to serve as a constant reminder to me that I was not my ideas, that they did not represent the voice of a fixed identity. The hope was that I would always remain detached, non–ego identified with the work. Since my spiritual practice required that I remain open, ever willing to change

114

and let go, I wanted to create a meditative distance between me and my writing. The use of another name created that distance and, although in those days I rarely used the name except when writing, it was a challenge.

Graduate school was difficult. I found most of my classes to be without passion or joy. And the rich intellectual life I had dreamed of seemed more and more to be a fantasy. The academy as I experienced it was essentially such a dishonest, disheartening place that I felt myself torn, pulled between the longing to walk a spiritual path that I often hoped would lead to a monastic vocation and the longing to lead a contemplative intellectual life. In my search for self-understanding, I came to rely more and more on spiritual teachers and their writing and felt less engaged with critical theory. Still, I wanted there to be a place in my life for theory and politics as well as spiritual practice. My quest was to find that place.

Influenced by Islamic mysticism to believe that my work must be in the world and not away from it, I began to think of ways to bring spiritual practice closer to the intellectual work I had chosen, and to infuse that intellectual work with a political vision of social transformation. When I discovered Thich Nhat Hanh and Daniel Berrigan's book of dialogues, *The Raft Is Not the Shore*, I learned from their shared wisdom. Their insistence that it was more significant to practice faith than to know doctrine or even to do all the right spiritual rituals was helpful to me. Nhat Hanh's thinking about self-recovery converged with my thoughts about the decolonization of black people and our collective efforts to engage in political self-recovery:

In the Buddhist tradition, people used to speak of enlighten-ment, as a kind of returning home. The three worlds—the world of form, of nonform, of desire—are not your homes.

These are places where you wander around for many exis-
tences, alienated from your own nature. So enlightenment
is the way to get back. And, they speak about efforts to go
back—described in terms of the recovery of oneself, of one's
integrity.

Using this vision of self-recovery to think about the struggles of
colonized people to make themselves subject, I began to see points
of convergence between the effort to live in the spirit and the effort
of oppressed people to renew their spirits, to find themselves again
in resistance. In my political writing, I began to draw together the
spiritual and the political.

After I finished my doctorate, I went to teach full-time at Yale
University, though I had already taught at several institutions. Yale
was special because the African-American culture center every
Sunday became a place for spiritual bonding. An interdenomina-
tional, traditional black church service took place there. Wor-
shippers were students, staff, faculty, and members from the
surrounding neighborhoods. Though it was often a small group, I
was reminded of the importance of community by participating
once again in collective spiritual worship. At black church, we
linked worship with the daily struggles of life in that academic
world. We worked to offer one another concrete practices that
would strengthen us as we worked to maintain spiritual practice in
an environment that overvalued the mind and the intellect. In
response to what I took to be the spiritual hunger of my students
and my own longings, I worked to create a critical pedagogy that
would enable students to use the knowledge and information
gained in the university to live more fully in the world, one that
would speak to heart, soul, mind, body, and spirit. Increasingly, I
found myself giving public voice to the spiritual practice that I had

been silent about. Giving a lay sermon at a Yale black church service during International Women's month, I found myself struggling to articulate my sense of spirituality, its meaning in my life. My talk was titled "Called to Love." In it I described my years of spiritual journeying in search of a particular doctrine and tradition I might claim and follow, the disappointment I felt when the attraction of no one faith moved me. After years of learning about different traditions, I found myself putting together bits and pieces from various religious teachings. The tie that bound them all together was the emphasis on Love as a transformative force, as the ultimate expression of godliness.

Letting my political and intellectual work be guided by an ethics of Love, I began to feel a harmony where there had been a sense of conflict. My quest was to express divine Love to the fullest in all my work. In this quest I have drawn from the writing of Martin Luther King Jr., who believed that the world would be healed by a "creative redemptive love." And despite the evil in this world, the hatred and alienation, King was able to maintain his belief that love was "ultimately the only answer" to all our problems. Giving his "Where do we go from here?" speech he could testify:

> I have decided to love. If you are seeking the highest good, I think you can find it through love. And the beautiful thing is that we are moving wrong when we do not do it because John was right, God is love. He who hates does not know God, but he who has love has the key that unlocks the door to the meaning of ultimate reality.

Fundamentally, the foundation of meaningful spiritual practice is a loving heart.

To be guided by Love in every action of daily life enables the individual to act politically and intellectually in a manner that embraces always a collective good. Once my comrade and friend Cornel West and I were discussing our committing to sharing the "word" in both a political and a spiritual sense, and we were talking about the issue of responsibility. I was reminded of the line in the song that Sweet Honey in the Rock sings, "When we work for freedom, we can rest." Cornel raised the issue of "sacrificial love," calling attention to the example of Jesus. Later I wrote these words to him in a letter:

> I was awake last night thinking about your comments on sacrificial love—which I believe begins with surrendering one's life to God. This surrender is the state of being through which and from which one serves, whether that service manifests as political organizing, writing, or teaching. It is this state of surrender that enables one to be in touch with divine will, so that it is not simply our choosing but god who chooses within us. That is the intimate solitary space of our submission where god speaks to us, where we are still, where we are truly "servants." In that still place, found in meditation, prayer, times of silence, I listen to my heart as I attempt to choose the direction of my work, the causes I support.

Living a life in the spirit, living faith, means that I must be ever vigilant, critically interrogating my actions, my words. Martin Luther King Jr. encouraged spiritual vigilance, confessing that "I subject myself to self-purification and to endless self-analysis; I question and soul-search constantly into myself to be as certain as I can that I am fulfilling the true meaning of my work. . . ." Often before I write or speak, I pray, asking in the words that I learned as a child that "the words of my mouth and the meditation of my heart be acceptable in thy sight." These moments of prayer remind me of my spiritual task. It is my hope and my experience that they temper the ego and deepen my compassion.

Thich Nhat Hanh has taught me much about the meaning of compassion. Through this teaching, I have found ways to under-stand and bear the isolation I often feel, the sense of exile. In *The Raft Is Not the Shore* he reminds us,

> I think that when you decide to do something in order to become yourself, and your thinking and your aspirations become one, you might find that you are quite alone. People will not understand; people will oppose you. A kind of lone-liness, a real exile settles in. You may be with your parents, with your friends, with your community, but you are in exile practically because of that situation.

Confronting myself with compassion, I learn to practice the art of forgiveness. I learn how to love myself in a way that strengthens my capacity to love others.

To understand the place of compassion and forgiveness in resis-tance struggle is important for any revolutionary movement. Unless such a movement is guided by profound Love, it will often embody the forces of evil and corruption that it may seek to change. This is why it has been so necessary for black liberation struggle in the United States to have been nurtured by the wisdom of both Martin Luther King Jr. and Malcolm X. Both men emphasized the power of Love. For King, it was often the love we direct outward to others, even our enemies; for Malcolm, it was the love we extend to ourselves. Authentic spiritual practice is not a naive experience. It does not lead one away from reality but allows us to accept the real more fully. It means that we recognize the reality of sin, that we think of it in relation to the notion of putting "asunder," estranging, alienating. And, fundamentally, it means that we are able to choose life over death and as a consequence of this choice are able to know compassion, offer forgiveness, and create the circumstances that make reconciliation possible.

Howard Thurman maintained that the experience of redemptive love was essential for individual self-actualization. Such love affirms. In *Growing Edge*, Thurman contends: "Whether he is a good person or a bad person, he is being dealt with at a point beyond all that is limiting, and all that is creative within him. He is dealt with at the core of his being and at that core he is touched and released." In much of his work, Howard Thurman cautions those of us who are concerned with radical social change not to allow our visions to conform to a pattern we seek to impose but rather to allow them to be "modeled and shaped in accordance to the innermost transformation that is going on" in our spirits.

To be guided by Love is to live in community with all life. A culture of domination like ours does not strive to teach individuals how to live in community. As a consequence, this must become a core practice for all of us who desire to transform society in ways that will bring justice, enable peace and well-being—learning to live in community. All too often, individuals think of community in terms of being with folks like themselves—same class, race, ethnicity, social standing, and the like. It is when we are able to empathize, feel with and for experiences that are not our own and may never be, that we come to know "how good and pleasant it is for brethren to come together in unity." To make community, we need to be able to know truth, to speak openly and honestly.

Truth-telling has to be a spiritual practice for many of us because we live and work in settings where falseness is rewarded, where lies are the norm. Deceit and betrayal destroy the possibility of community. In challenging the separation of public and private in feminist activism, or any struggle of the exploited to move from object being to subject being, we act to restore the idea that meaningful ties, bonds of love and affinity, are fruitful in a world beyond domestic reality. Strengthening our capacity to offer a sense of community to those who are different, we prepare to dwell in that deeper community that is based on shared vision. I am moved when Nhat Hanh shares: "I want to express my hope in the community of people who have the same concerns and who are working for the same goals. What helps individuals in the community is your doing the same things I do, in your own way. I can learn from you." Or when Sharon Welch emphasizes the call for unity in *Communities of Resistance and Solidarity*, explaining what solidarity means in relation to Christian practice: "Solidarity breaks the bonds of isolated individuality and forgetfulness—the bondage of sin—and enables the creation of community and conversion to the other." In my political writing and other forms of activism, I endeavor to evoke, build, and sustain a sense of community that I see most strongly developed in theory and practice by religious and/or spiritual people. Those of us who would transform society have much to learn from studying black liberation struggles in the United States. For throughout the history of black freedom movements, the prime movers and shakers have been individuals committed to a life in the spirit.

In recent years, I have chosen to speak publicly about spirituality and spiritual practice because so many of the young people I teach are often overwhelmed by feelings of hopelessness and despair. They have been that group of individuals in my life who most want to know what sustains me, what allows me to keep the faith. And I have answered them openly and honestly. I share with them the meaning of spirituality in my life. I live my life in a manner that I trust embodies the ideas, beliefs, and values I write about. Perhaps one of the most intense political struggles we face as individuals seeking to transform society today is the effort to maintain integrity of being. In my letter to Cornel I wrote,

> We bear witness not just with our intellectual work but with ourselves, our lives. Surely the crisis of these times demands that we give our all. Remember the song which asks, "Is your all on the altar of sacrifice laid?" To me, this "all" includes our habits of being, the way we live. It is both political practice and religious sacrament—a life of resistance. How can we speak of change, of hope, and love, if we court death? All the work we do, no matter how brilliant or revolutionary in thought or action, loses power and meaning if we lack integrity of being.

I can testify that meaningful spiritual practice sustains and nurtures progressive politics, that it enhances the struggle for liberation, that it allows that integrity of being to surface in settings where we are sorely tempted to move against our vows and beliefs. As Gustavo Gutierrez proclaims, "A spirituality of liberation will center on a *conversion* to the neighbor, the oppressed person, the exploited social class, the despised race, the dominated country. . . . *Conversion* means a radical transformation of ourselves. . . . To be converted is to commit oneself to the process of the liberation of poor and oppressed, to commit oneself lucidly, realistically, and concretely." Hear again the call for concrete action, for a radical faith realized in deeds.

Balancing the inner spiritual journey with our struggle to work in the world requires ongoing practice. Often when I am uncertain about where to stand politically, when I feel that I may not be seeing clearly, I read from Psalms 139, especially that passage which says, "Search me, Oh God and know my heart: try me and know my thoughts." I have tried here in this writing to speak of the way spiritual inner movement flows outward, the way the fire within burns with an intensity that brings light, vision, warmth to every aspect of my being. It is this sacred fire that can be felt in my writing. Anyone who has known the sweet communion of holy spirits, the ecstasy of divine love knows how difficult it is to give such experience words. To me, these words that I have written, a confession of my faith, are necessary testimony even though they can never name religious experience fully. I have wanted simply to locate that meeting-place of spirituality and progressive politics in my life.

divine inspiration

writing and spirituality

In the town I grew up in on hot summer nights when nature was in still repose, it was possible to wander down a narrow unpaved street following the sounds of a tent meeting. It was possible to hear the sounds of voices moved by spirits—voices caught in moments of divine rapture. As children of a more conservative faith, we were not allowed to attend Pentecostal meetings. I went once. My best friend's family were all "holy rollers" as they were often called. And I was allowed to attend with her, even though I was given strict instructions to maintain myself. In other words I was not to allow myself to surrender to the call of divine rapture. I was not to be moved by unseen spirits.

The spirits were there in the tent that night. I could hear and feel them. To my friend who had always attended holiness meetings, there was nothing special or exciting about watching worshipers shout or speak in tongues. But I was mesmerized. Awed to be a witness to mystery. I only saw and heard it once yet the expressions of religious ecstasy and shared rapture stirred my soul. I came away believing more deeply than ever before in a mystical force in the universe—a force that had the power to call us, to touch us with divine spirit.

Baptized as a girl in the church of my upbringing in the "name of the father, the son, and the holy spirit" I soon became enthralled by the mystical dimensions of religious life. On my way to becoming a feminist thinker, writer, and cultural critic I walked farther and farther away from father and son, but my steps always drew me closer to holy spirit. Its presence could never be rejected or denied. Everywhere I turned in nature I could see and feel the mystery—the wonder of that which could not be accounted for by human reason.

Spirituality has always been the foundation of my experience as a writer. Most writers know that our visions often emerge from places that are mysterious—far removed from who we are and what we think we know. Faced with this reality again and again as we work with words, we can only acknowledge the presence of an unseen force. Encountering this force was my earliest understanding of what was meant by the evocation of "grace." In my home church we would sing, "Grace woke me up this morning—grace started me on my way." This grace was understood as a recognition of the presence of mystery. We trust from childhood on that we can sleep and wake, that we can rise, that our open eyes will see. For many of us this trust is our covenant with godliness—our appreciation of the mystery of holiness.

In Buddhist practice when we learn to be mindfully aware of our actions in everyday life we are essentially learning to practice spiritual vigilance in such a way that we can actually hear the sounds of mystery. Once our daily actions are infused with a sense of the sacred, we hear the rhythms of grace. Like a silent chant those rhythms help steady the mind and bring us peace. If we are listening and moving with these rhythms every action we take, from rising out of bed to cleaning ourselves, preparing meals, and so forth, reveals to us the sacredness of all life.

Writing has been for me one of the ways to encounter the divine. As a discipline of mind and heart working with words has become a spiritual practice. Steeped in Christian faith, throughout my young adulthood I would fall on my knees to pray for the "right words"— for an integrity of mind and heart that would lead me to right livelihood in my work with words. Oftentimes I would repeat a prayer that would include the scriptural admonition to "let the words of my mouth and the meditation of my heart be acceptable." Initially, even though I prayed for divine guidance about my work, I was not really wholeheartedly willing to follow a path that was not in tune with my desires. Ultimately, the conditions of my surrender were not complex; my desires often simply did not work. When I gave myself over to the writing I felt called to do, I experienced fulfillment.

My vision of the writing I would do was informed by a longing to give expression to an inner emotional universe that was mostly self-referential. I began my writing career believing I would be a poet, a bohemian, avant-garde, art-for-art's-sake writer. All the writing classes I took focused on poetry. My engagement with Buddhism began with poets and poetry. Yet it was the struggle to find my voice as a poet that led me to feminist thinking and feminist politics. Even though I continued to write poetry as I prayed and meditated about my writing future I felt called to write a book about black women and feminism. It is difficult to explain the nature of this calling—what it means to be called by that unseen force I call divine grace.

During this period of struggle I heard voices calling to me in my dreams, telling me that it was important for me to speak about the experience of black women. My maternal grandmother and great-grandmothers were figures in my dream life urging me to answer this call, telling me that they would help direct my path. Despite my initial resistance I would sit at my desk and find myself seemingly without will, writing just what the voices were telling me to write about.

Imagine my distress when I answered the call of these voices and committed myself to writing work only to find that writing mocked, that no one wanted to publish it. I was confused. Naively thinking that answering the call of unseen forces would somehow work like magic to ensure the success of my writing, I confronted the reality that we may discover the rightness of our vision and vocation before others do. I wish that I could confess that my faith was so great I did not despair. Indeed, I did. It was with a heavy heart that I took this first manuscript of mine and stored it away in a closet. I took it out again when I accepted more fully that completing the book was my path to fulfillment. Whether or not it would ever be published was another question altogether.

The serendipitous way that my first book found its publishers seemed to confirm the presence of unseen spirits. I had mentioned to a new friend I met when she was waiting on tables at a museum café that I was working on this book. When we spent time together I shared what it was about. It was she who called to say that she had seen a small ad in a newspaper calling for manuscripts about race and feminism. That ad was placed by South End Press, who would publish this book of mine and many more.

Writing and publishing my first book was a long-drawn-out test of faith. It was a process that taught me patience. It intensified my awareness that knowing the path we want to take does not mean that it will not be an arduous one or that the difficulty of the journey means potential failure. During this process I not only reaffirmed my commitment to spiritual practice; devotion to this path enhanced my commitment to writing and my ability to write.

Not much is written about the connection between writing and spirituality. Even though New Age writing describes circumstances where writers receive ideas mysteriously, rarely does anyone talk about the sustained link between spiritual practice and writing. Writers are reluctant to speak about this subject because literary elitism engenders a fear that if we describe "unseen forces" shaping our visions and the structure of our writing we will not be taken seriously. Women writers have been more willing than their male counterparts to speak of visions that serve as a catalyst for the imaginative process. When describing the process of writing *The Color Purple*, Alice Walker spoke of images appearing in her dreams, of voices, of spirits calling to her.

Oftentimes men have evoked the muse, whether real or fictive, to talk about those forces beyond the realm of human reason that drive the imagination. Since the male muse was so often imagined as an obscure object of desire, usually a beautiful young female being but sometimes male, this has always been an acceptable way to talk about "spirits" and the creative imagination. Few men attempt to link their muses to spiritual practice. Indeed, the Beat poets in their own rebellious anti-establishment way were among the first modern writers to unabashedly mesh together the spiritual and transgressive creative process.

It was this unlikely pairing that drew me to the Beat poets. In 1959 Kerouac would tell the world that the heartbeat of his transgressive spirit was triggered in the traditional church. Sharing his perspective on the origin of the Beat perspective he declared: "Yet it was as a Catholic, it was not at the insistence of any of these 'niks' and certainly not with their approval either, that I went one afternoon to the church of my childhood (one of them), Ste. Jeanne d'Arc in Lowell Mass., and suddenly with tears in my eyes and had a vision of what I must have really meant with 'Beat' anyhow when I heard the holy silence in the church . . . the vision of the word Beat as being to mean beatific. . . ." Kerouac's transition to Buddhism was engendered by grief from lost love. To cope with his suffering he began reading *The Life of Buddha* by Ashvagosa.

I follow the path Kerouac helped forge as I work to mesh my intense Christian upbringing with Buddhist thought. In the late sixties he continued to work through the convergences between these two spiritual paths, juxtaposing Christian teachings with Buddhist writing. Starting with the assumption that "words come from the holy ghost" Kerouac reminded readers that "Mozart and Blake often felt they weren't pushing their own pens, 'twas the 'Muse' singing and pushing."

When I sit down to write I do not imagine my pen will be guided by anything other than the strength of my will, imagination, and intellect. When the spirit moves into that writing, shaping its direction, that is for me a moment of pure mystery. It is a visitation of the sacred that I cannot call forth at will. I can only hope it will come. This hope is grounded in my own experience that in those moments when I feel my imagination and the words I put together to be touched by the presence of divine spirit my writing is transformed. At such moments I am touched by grace. I am moved both by the writing and by the presence of spirits that make that writing the very best that it can be. When I complete this work I feel intense jubilation and ecstasy. Not all the writing I do is divinely inspired. The difference is tangible. Many writers who have felt guided by unseen spirits testify that the writing poured forth with ease. Much of the time we labor over words.

More than anything my writing is informed by spiritual practice in relation to the subjects I choose to write about. After my first book I have never written any other without first spending significant time in prayer and meditation about content and the direction of work. Since I always have many ideas, I count on sacred visitation to guide me to the timeliness of work. My reliance on spiritual guidance is connected to the desire I have for the writing to touch the hearts of readers—to speak to their innermost being. Much of my work is written to create a context of healing. Words have the power to heal wounds. Out of the mysterious place where words first come to be "made flesh"—that place which is all holiness—I am given the grace to work with words in a spirit of right livelihood that calls me to peace, reflection, and connectedness with communities of readers whom I may never know or see. Writing becomes then a way to embrace the mysterious, to walk with spirits, and an entry into the realm of the sacred.

intellectual life

in and beyond the academy

Every writer dreams of writing compelling work that will be read, understood, and appreciated. Many writers do not dream of publication or of writing a best-seller. Most do not imagine ever making money from their work. I often feel that there is a world of difference between life experiences of individuals whose vocation is clear to them in childhood and the life experiences of those folks who must search to discover what it is they want to do in life. I knew that I wanted to be a writer as a child. Grown black folks in our household were not that moved by my longings because they did not know any black person who made a living as a writer. They wanted me to be able to take care of myself. The best way for a southern black working-class girl to do that was to become a schoolteacher. Dutifully I went to college to prepare myself to make a living. There is nothing magical about my choice to study English. I loved to read. Studying literature was a way to read and still be on a path that would lead to a job. My class background was such that I did not think about a career. I thought about a job, work that would pay the rent, put food on the table.

Before me, my mother had loved reading books and dreamed of becoming a writer. Like her, I began to write by creating poems. When my first book was published the dedication read: "For Rosa Bell, my mother—who told me when I was a child that she had once written poems—that I had inherited my love of reading and my longing to write from her." My mother married as a teenager. She had many babies, one right after the other. She kept house, cooked, cleaned, and nurtured our dreams. Every now and then she worked outside the home as a maid in the houses of white women. Mostly, we lived off the steady income my father received from his job as a janitor at the post office. As children we knew that our mother was beautiful and wonderfully creative—a worker of magic. If you had dreams and longings you could take them to her and she would chart the path to fulfillment. She did this so well that it was only when I was far away from home, a scholarship student at Stanford University, that I began to think critically about her life. In my first women's studies course, our visiting professor Tillie Olsen, a writer from a working-class background, shared the hardships of trying to make a living, raise children, and write. It was in this class that I first began to think about the dreams my mother had sacrificed as the daily demands of raising seven children and caring for our father's every whim consumed her time and energy. It was in this class that I began to think critically about feminism and black womanhood. It was a turning point. Shortly after this class ended, I began to write my first book. I was nineteen years old. Ten years later it was published. By then, I fully understood the gift my working-class mother had given to me in choosing to share her dream.

Initially, I received no money for writing this first book. It was not written for money or fame. It was a pure and passionate expression of my longing to create a space within feminist movement for the voices and visions of black women. This task accomplished, I still needed a job. I went to graduate school to become an English professor. In graduate school my passion for ideas and writing intensified. Yet, I still continued to think of teaching as a job, not as a career. Writing was my true vocation. Teaching was a way for me to continue to write. By the time I finished my doctorate in English at the University of California, I had published my first book and was writing a new work. The career I had begun to pursue in the academy was secondary.

By the time I was hired to be an assistant professor at Yale University in African-American studies and English, I was constantly walking a tightrope, trying to fulfill the requirements that would lead to tenure while searching for the space to write. The conventional literary criticism that I wrote and published as part of professional expectations did not interest me as much as the polemical essays I continued to write on issues relating to feminism. The wide-ranging, often random, interdisciplinary reading I did provided the intellectual backdrop for my development as a feminist thinker, as did the ongoing debates and discussions I had with other feminist scholars. Early on, there was so little critical work that addressed issues in black life from a feminist standpoint that it was incredibly exciting to be among those women active in feminist movement daring to investigate aspects of our life experiences rendered invisible by race, sex, and class biases. We saw our work in feminist theory as breaking new ground, as cutting-edge. We were trying to create paradigms that would enable us to understand gender from standpoints that would be inclusive of race, gender, and class. Writing progressive feminist theory was so compelling precisely because we knew that the work we were doing, if it was at all useful, would have a meaningful transformative impact on our lives and the lives of women and men both inside and outside the academy. While consistently critiquing the racism of white women within the women's movement, the way racist standpoints shaped their critical writing on gender, my primary concern was providing analysis and strategies that would enable black women to constructively engage feminism. With messianic zeal, I worked hard to do work that would both illuminate the impact of sexism on the social status of black women and speak to the relevance of feminist movement in black life. In keeping with my politics, I published my books at South End Press, a progressive left publishing collective. I chose them, instead of seeking a larger corporate press that would have given advances and paid royalties consistently, because the women and men at SEP were committed to feminist movement, to ending domination in all its forms—racism, classism, imperialism, etc. None of us made a lot of money. For years, the press struggled to survive, to faithfully pay royalties when the money was there. South End Press was and remains committed to publishing progressive ideas that advance the cause of justice. In the early days, the issue was rarely whether a book would sell but whether it would advance a meaningful cause. This was the perfect union of politics and vocation.

In the academic world, my colleagues were not impressed by books published by South End Press. This was not a press that had status and prestige. In their eyes it was not "legitimately" academic. After all, those folks were willing to publish books without footnotes, that did not abide by the rules of the MLA style sheet. South End Press was publishing books for the people, trying to bridge the gap between the academy and the world outside. As an intellectual and writer eager to share knowledge, to educate for critical consciousness, I shared this vision. When we began to work together, none of us had any idea that my work would begin to have a powerful impact on feminist thinking, that it would be used in college classrooms throughout the United States, that in time it would actually make money for both the press and me, not a huge sum but more than I had ever imagined receiving from critical writing. Since I had made my steady income as a professor, I was not that concerned with whether the books made money. The blessing that came was that the books were read, understood, and appreciated. As a direction of feminist theory shifted, and race became central to the discussion, my work became more relevant. My voice and the voices of other black women/women of color were not only gaining a hearing, we were changing the nature of the discourse.

Feminist movement and women's studies have been the foundation of my success as a writer and a critical thinker. The seven books I wrote and published with South End were faithfully bought and studied by a progressive audience, composed primarily of feminist readers. Their responses to the work, both critical and celebratory, inspired me to keep writing. These days mainstream interest in the critical writings of black academics/intellectuals has shined a spotlight on "bell hooks" that is quite different from the warm critical engagement that has consistently radiated from that core group of progressive readers who study my work. Ironically, the growing number of press clippings that talk about black intellectuals, that highlight "bell hooks" say little or nothing about my work. Rarely is the word *feminism* uttered. Articles that say something about the rising star of "bell hooks" place me first and foremost in a discussion that is usually taking place between men about men. I am a token, a nod in the direction of political "correctness." In his recent polemical attack "What Are the Drums Saying, Booker: The Current Crisis of the Black Intellectual" published in *The Village Voice*, Adolph Reed included me in his ballistic trashing, making only two observations, neither based on any facts. He claimed that Cornel West and I "gush over each other's brilliance," and that I am a hustler, "blending bombast, cliches, psychobabble, and lame guilt tripping in service to the 'pay me' principle." He never mentions the word *feminism*. The fact that it is feminism that has been the force that catapulted me onto the critical scene and not white mania for black intellectuals would deflect away from his representation of me as one in a long line of darky minstrels working overtime to catch massa's eye. Reed's backhand "diss" of me and my work is nothing new. He is dancing perfectly in step with the way mainstream male-dominated discourse about "black intellectuals" has consistently represented me. In the review of my latest books in the *New York Times*, which for years ignored my work completely, the white male scholar began by identifying me as "the friend of Cornel West." As though West is the Lone Ranger and I am Tonto. Everything he said about the work was confined to the introduction. Unlike other books by feminist writers reviewed in the *Times*, which are usually critiqued by feminist thinkers, or at least someone whose discipline and/or interest suggests some knowledge of the field discussed, the two times my work has been given cursory negative review in the *Times*, it has been by writers who have come out of nowhere, who have no interest in either feminist theory or cultural criticism. Of course, I only began to receive reviews in the *Times* after several articles appeared in other journals pointing out that they tended to ignore my work and that of other black thinkers on the left, with the exception being Cornel West. This is the type of affirmative-action tokenism that one could do without.

That same spirit of inclusive tokenism is present in a *New Yorker* piece by Michael Berube titled "Public Academy." Underneath the title there is this declaration: "A new generation of black thinkers is becoming the most dynamic force in the American intellectual arena since the fifties." Berube, in what is essentially a series of book reviews, frames his piece as an overview of the impact of black intellectuals. That impact is registered not by the significance of our work but rather in terms of our current popularity, particularly in relation to the books he is reviewing. While Berube does not acknowledge any relation between my "public intellectual" work and feminist movement, he does register that feminism is a major topic of my writing. On all matters in the two recent books of mine he writes about, Berube finds me engaging in "sweeping indiscriminate critique" with the exception being my critical thoughts on feminism. He contends that I am at my "best in debates over the meaning and future of feminism." Of course, part of white male privilege is that he is in no way required to contextualize his basis for judgment and evaluation. Not only was I the token woman in the piece, I was apparently the only thinker whose ideas Berube vehemently disagreed with, so much so that a fellow black woman writer commented that I am represented as the irrational "strident lunatic." Of course, the irony of this piece is that the books he reviews do not represent the type of work I have done within women's studies that has made a meaningful critical intervention. A similar overview of the work of black intellectuals published in the *LA Weekly* made no mention of my work even though I spent hours with reporter Sam Fullwood talking "ideas." His agenda seems to have been sifting through our extensive conversation to ferret out critical comments about Cornel West. As in other instances, the focus of attention is really on a public discourse about black intellectuals that is taking place between black men.

When *The Chronicle of Higher Education* sent Courtney Leatherman, a white woman reporter, to interview me, I hoped to finally engage in a discussion that would focus more on ideas. At no point in our conversation, which went on for hours, did the reporter indicate that she was working on a cover story. After hours of discussing "ideas," Leatherman was welcomed to stay for lunch and observe other parts of my life. When her piece appeared as the cover story in a May issue of the newspaper, ideas were not mentioned. While I consistently shared with Leatherman that I did not consider myself a "black feminist" but rather an advocate of feminist politics her cover story carried the heading "A Name for Herself: When black feminism needed a voice, bell hooks was born." Apparently, Leatherman's tape recorder lost the part where I shared that I had begun to use the name bell hooks long before I became involved with feminist movement. Indeed, there are so many lies and distortions of our conversation in her piece that it was mind-boggling.

There was no evidence of a discussion of feminist politics and ideas, only anecdotal references to the details shared during lunch. Many colleagues had called me to share their perception that Leatherman was clearly fishing for dirt to use in her tabloid-like piece. Evidently, not finding the necessary dirt she painted a colorful imaginative portrait gleaned more from her stereotypes and fantasies. I first heard that the piece had been published when interviewed by a reporter from the *Times Educational Supplement* (London). When I asked about the piece she frowned and commented: "She seemed not to have read any of your work." This refusal to critically consider the work characterizes much of the mainstream public attention I am now receiving. For most of my writing life, I had not been open to talking with the press, to having photos taken. It was the desire to reach a wider audience that motivated me to be more open. This has been a mixed blessing. On one hand, the attention increases the number of readers who know that the work exists. It enables me to seek advances, which I never had for the earlier work. On the other hand, it often misrepresents both me and the work.

Since much of the work I have done in the last few years within feminist theory as well as cultural studies has focused on the significance of representation within structures of domination, the impact of images as they reinforce racist and sexist stereotypes, I am painfully aware of the ways my image is now used to undermine the academic work I am most committed to doing. In part, I see the misrepresentation of this work as part of an overall antifeminist backlash within mass media, where the work of progressive feminist thinkers is often distorted and made to appear trivial or ridiculous. When individual women set themselves up as "thought police" monitoring the feminist classroom and reporting back to the mainstream world its problems and excesses, few uninformed readers speculate as to why it is the feminist classroom that is under surveillance and not other pedagogical settings. Indeed, if every academic discipline were subject to the harsh scrutiny with which critics examine both women's studies and other nontraditional programs and departments we would all be compelled to acknowledge that all disciplines have their teachers who are flawed, biased, and protective of their space. Concurrently, since I have strayed from the traditional academic path and continued to pursue writing as a primary vocation and teaching as a job, a choice made evident by my attempt, after first doing the traditional training and scholarship common to my discipline, to write for a more general audience, I am an easy target to critique for conservatives who want there to be homogeneous thought and action among professors in specific disciplines.

For some time now, I have felt the scope of critical thinking and writing by black Americans threatened by the fact that practically all black writers seek some type of affiliation with academic institutions for sustained employment. It is precisely because common structures of evaluation and advancement in various academic jobs require homogeneous thought and action, judged usually from a conservative standpoint, that academia is often less a site for open-minded creative study and engagement with ideas and more a space of repression that dissenting voices are so easily censored and/or silenced. Within the academy, individuals from marginalized groups are more likely to be subject to a quality of scrutiny that curtails freedom of speech and thought. This is one reason it is dangerous for us to allow academic institutions to remain the primary site where our ideas are developed and exchanged.

Since my undergraduate years I have longed to leave the academy. For years I have tried to live modestly so that I can one day survive without having to work as an academic. In the last few years that has been possible, but I stay in the academy in part because I want students to know the value of education and to believe that they can have critical consciousness even as they work within existing structures to gain knowledge and prepare themselves for a life where much of their time will be spent working. I believe that as a working-class black girl growing up in the racial apartheid of Hopkinsville, Kentucky, I would not be doing the work I do, the thinking and writing I love, were it not for the many neighbors (mostly older black women) who gave me literature to read that broadened my horizons and the teachers and librarians who enabled me to pursue my longing for knowledge. Their generosity was an example to me. I endeavor to teach students that same generosity and care. Like my teachers, I do not simply hope that students will learn necessary facts and details. I hope that they will learn to think critically in ways that strengthen their capacity to be self-actualized.

Much of the writing I do is grounded in my ongoing political commitment to ending domination in all its forms. I remain particularly concerned about the struggles to end racism and sexism. The way I write (style, content), the choices I make regarding subject matter reflect these commitments. Concurrently, I try to preserve a place of creativity where I can think and write on any subject, irrespective of whether it will enhance freedom struggle globally. It takes effort to lead a balanced creative and intellectual life. There are so many aspects of black and/or female experience that have never been explored.

Sometimes I think we need progressive educational centers in every state to nurture the production of ideas about groups for whom discrimination and unjust distribution of resources (and that includes education) has left huge gaps in our understanding. It is the desire to think and write more, to fill some of these gaps that informs my desire to leave the academy—to think and write on the subjects of my choice, in the manner that I wish to write, in whatever voice I choose. There is so much emphasis on asserting a one-dimensional "voice" in academic life. I enjoy writing about many subjects in different ways. Not only is this a way to claim decolonized subjectivity, it enriches my capacity for self-actualization. I hope that students will know the way to do formal academic writing and other ways of writing if they wish to have a broader audience. The intellectual life I have chosen is rewarding and deeply satisfying. I began to talk more about the blessings such a life can bring because it seemed to me that by only calling attention to the pitfalls of academic life, I and other colleagues were not setting a good example for students and peers.

To me intellectual life is fundamentally different from academic careerism. I feel especially fortunate that I have been able to pursue an academic career in which I have had to make minimal compromise to achieve my desired goals. By the standards of academic careerism, it is not a sign of major achievement to be teaching in a huge urban state college that is predominantly non-white. Indeed, prominent black academics shared with me their sense that I would be sabotaging my career to make such a move. I came to teach at a state college after years of teaching at two private institutions—Yale and Oberlin. My choice was informed by a desire to spend the years I have left in academia working with students of color, many of whom come from class backgrounds similar to my own. These are students who are often deemed unimportant by academic elites. Indeed, when Courtney Leatherman interviewed me she spent time with an undergraduate student I had encouraged to take my graduate class. Though Leatherman talked with this student, who is a black immigrant from a working-class background who works full-time to support herself while attending school, in her eagerness to paint a portrait of me as this seductive teacher whose students are slaves of love, Leatherman never mentions her conversation with this student. She quotes students from Yale and Oberlin, all of whom were dismayed by the way she mocked them and distorted the information they shared with her. All the students who talked with her were able to experience firsthand the power of mass media to distort truth, to misrepresent-represent them. Although I have received much mainstream attention this past year, this piece was the only instance where a reporter aggressively distorted information and at times just lied.

My initial response was to critique myself for being so open, for being willing to talk to the press. Then Dennis Green, at the time a black male colleague at City College teaching a course on the media and representation, reminded me that given the intactness of systems of domination, if I and the work I do were merely being celebrated in the press it would be a cause for alarm. As he put it, "You would need to look at yo'self and ask what I am doing wrong." Given the mounting backlash of conservative forces, covert and overt attacks on freedom of speech, this is a time when dissenting progressive voices both in and outside the academy need to cherish the spaces of open dialogue, the audiences that enable us to publish—to gain material reward, and most importantly, to have the joy of knowing our voices are heard and welcomed.

catalyst and connection

writers and readers

Writers rarely talk about the value of a reading audience. We like to imagine that we would all be merrily writing away even if there was no public longing to hear our words. I began my writing as a poet. Like most poets in a society where poetry is most often read silently and in private, I never imagined an audience for my poems. They were written to be read by me to a few intimate souls equally enchanted by lyricism. I was never compelled to take the stage at poetry readings nor was I inclined to scatter copies of my poems around for various readers to partake of them. Yet when I became engaged with feminist thinking and feminist movement the questions of whom we speak to and for became paramount.

Anyone writing feminist theory at the peak of contemporary feminist movement considered the question of audience. Critical interventions by women of color called attention to the politics of location and the question of perspective. In my early work I critiqued the ways in which the words chosen to talk about feminist movement indicated that when the category woman was evoked it was made synonymous with white women; that when feminist theorists talked about commonalities between women and blacks black women were excluded from the former. The challenge that all progressive feminist theorists faced was to find a language that could give expression to the specificity of experience and yet remain inclusive. We were all accustomed to using language in ways that perpetuated existing structures of domination, hierarchies of race, sex, and class.

Initially, I was primarily motivated to write feminist theory that would critique racism within feminist movement and call attention to sexism in black life along with the need to eradicate it. To achieve both these desired ends I had to formulate complex accountings for the intersections of race and gender, which needed unconventional forms of expression. I had to write with the trust that there would be readers willing to hear these different wordings, as well as the new insights they conveyed. When I wrote my first book *Ain't I a Woman: Black Women and Feminism,* I chose the subtitle with the direct intention of linguistically connecting our experience with feminist politics. Even though it had already become popular to speak of "black feminism" I chose not to use this phrase precisely because I did not want to support the notion of a racially distinct and separate-but-equal feminism. I wanted to make it clear that black women were primary to the making of feminist theory for everyone.

While I specifically wanted to address black women with this first book, I knew as well that racism and sexism directly targeted at us would never change if dominant groups (men and white women) did not learn more about black female experience. At that time, the vast majority of books about feminism were written by and about white women. The fact that these texts all focused on the experiences of a select group did not prevent me from learning from them.

Concurrently, white women and other groups eager to learn about black female experience were open to reading the feminist theory I wrote. At times it provoked in readers many different feelings—anger, sadness, guilt, etc.—but they grappled with the material. Often I meet readers who tell me that they found a book of mine so disturbing that they had to put it away or that they kept getting mad and throwing it in the trash but that something would always make them return to it. Writing that addresses audiences in a new way provokes.

Sadly, we are moving further and further away from the revolutionary feminist call for an inclusive approach to feminist thinking and writing that we dreamed would ultimately transform all writing in our culture. Nowadays it is often assumed that if a black woman writer of nonfiction concentrates on black experience and/or race, she is only writing for black female readers. Of course the irony is that a white woman can concentrate solely on white experience and/or race and she will be perceived as writing a book for a general audience. Racism creates a mindset that allows everyone to see white experience as the "norm," "the universal," and more particularly as the most significant. This last aspect is most important. It creates profound blind spots as it does not allow for the possibility that understanding black female experience might illuminate in a complex manner the experiences of white and other nonblack women or that these groups might learn vital information that would be meaningful for their lives. A perfect example of this is the way in which women of color, in particular black women, insist that white women active in feminist thinking and feminist movement confront the issue of racism. This intervention truly transformed feminist scholarship and gave renewed energy to contemporary activism.

Although a book may specifically address the particular experi-

ence of any group it can have meaningful resonance for folks outside the group. Throughout my involvement in feminist movement
even when I was most adamantly challenging the racism in the
theory and practice, I was sharing that I had also learned so much
from reading the work of white women peers and nonblack women
of color. In a short essay I wrote for *The Chronicle of Higher Education*
I critiqued the reluctance or refusal on the part of some women students to read male writers they deemed sexist; black students doing
the same when they considered a writer racist, etc. I was not urging
students to ignore the blind spots biases create but rather to both
critically interrogate them while also taking from a work the ideas
and beliefs that transcend those biases. Of course nonwhite readers
are always being challenged to look beyond the biases of white writers to appreciate the substance of their work, yet rarely are white
readers encouraged to believe they should do the same if the writer
is nonwhite.

Even when a work by a nonwhite writer is in no way biased yet
specifically addresses nonwhite experience, it is likely to be seen by
mainstream culture as irrelevant to white readers. The one book I
wrote specifically addressed to black women is a discussion of the
politics of self-recovery titled *Sisters of the Yam: Black Women and
Self-Recovery*. When it was first read by the alternative collective that
was publishing most of my work, they shared their concern that
there might be no audience for such a book. Like most predominately white publishing spaces they thought that the primary consumers of their books were a white reading public. I vehemently
challenged this assumption while also insisting that it would be
crucial that white people and other nonblack people read work illu-
minating black experience. In the same way I believe it essential
that black people read work that illuminates the experiences of all
other nonblack groups. All black people educated in this society

read and study work that illuminates white experience, even though whiteness is rarely overtly named. The politics of white supremacy allow the experiences of white people, usually those who have some degree of class privilege, to count as normal—as universal.

This thinking prevails in the publishing industry. Books that focus specifically on issues relating to black people written by black writers, especially authors who are not associated with predominately white institutions, tend to be seen as being only for a black audience. Publicity for these works will usually be most visible in publications that cater to black audiences. There are definitely some black writers who are only or most interested in attracting black readers. However, the vast majority of black writers, like most authors, want to attract a wide reading audience. In an animated conversation with a white female publishing executive about manuscripts, I shared that I was planning to write a book about women and midlife. She wanted to know if it was a book for black women or was it about, as she put it, "people like me." She never stated that she meant white women. I inquired as to what she meant; she replied that she wanted to know if it was for a general audience. Nothing I shared indicated a lack of an interest in a general audience. Indeed, I had used the phrase "women and midlife."

Although my manuscript looks at the experiences of women across race and class, I was reminded of all the books I had read about menopause that only address the experiences of white women but are represented as being about the experiences of "women." I doubt that any publishing executives attempt to steer writing by white women in a more inclusive direction; they don't have to. Black and other nonwhite consumers are accustomed to buying books that do not directly address us, but clearly there are shared experiences that cut across the boundaries of race. I constantly learn from books written by and about white women. If those books contain racial biases I critique them even as I benefit from the substantive information they contain. A work is not racist simply because it is by and about white women. An underlying covert racism operates when the experiences of white women are represented as synonymous with those of all women. In worst-case scenarios, if only the experiences of white women are studied as a way of comprehending female experience then our knowledge always remains faulty—inadequate and incomplete. These were the concerns raised by the most visionary thinkers in contemporary feminism. As a powerful corrective they changed the perspective of a wide range of women thinkers across race and class. As a consequence there have been significant changes in the expectations and taste of women readers.

Readers of books are much more open-minded than the publishing industry, including critics and reviewers, imagines. While my work has received relatively few reviews in the mainstream press, it is usually described as though it does not address a general audience or is in some way incomprehensible for readers who are not black. Despite these reviews a general audience of readers buys my work. And the bulk of letters I receive indicate that readers who are not black or female have no difficulty identifying with and/or understanding the experiences described. In conversation a young white woman editor who loves the memoir of my girlhood shared that she told another white woman peer that she had given a copy to a Latina woman who also loved it. This woman was surprised that nonblack readers enjoy the book. Surely, she would not be surprised to find that Latina, Asian, or black readers enjoy and identify with works by white writers.

As I often write work that challenges received understanding of subjects like race, gender, and class, it has been enormously helpful for me to receive feedback from readers. Often readers suggest subjects that they would like to see me write about or express interest in a subject that I want to write about but had my interest dampened by someone in publishing who suggested that the topic is not compelling. Encouragement received from readers inspires me. Before I published books I did not really think that much about reader response. Yet when any writer does work that is provocative and not well received by the mainstream world of critics and reviewers, the fact that the work is often misunderstood or misread can be so depressing that it can inhibit the creative process. At times when I have felt deeply discouraged, affirmative reader response has been one of the factors enabling me to continue to write.

In conjunction with letters received, teaching and lecturing has kept me in constant dialogue with a reading public. Often I am enabled to talk about topics I intend to write about before I begin writing. When individuals respond by urging me to pursue a given topic as they desperately want to read such a book, it is another affirmative reminder that I am on the right track. That reminder can be particularly important if the publishing world is not very enthusiastic about the project. This was certainly the case when I first talked with my editor at Routledge about a book on teaching. He expressed concern about the relevance of the topic. Once again the question of audience was raised. From my perspective as a professor I knew how often teachers and students expressed confusion about the teaching and learning experience, particularly when it came to talking about issues of freedom of speech in the classroom, how to cope with differences, etc. And I felt strongly that a book talking about these issues would be well received. That was the groundwork that became the catalyst for the collection of essays on teaching *Teaching to Transgress: Education as the Practice of Freedom*. There was an overwhelmingly positive reception for this work. I had not considered its potential to speak to audiences of educators who did not do university teaching since the essays were all focused on that setting. The relevance of the issues talked about to a wide and diverse audience was made clear by reader response. Readers were just incredibly passionate about this work, once again reminding me that the conservatism of the industry can be challenged and changed by writers and/or consumers.

Dialogues between readers and writers can challenge cynical notions about consumers. These conversations take place in diverse locations through the mail, at lectures and public readings. Bookstore readings are one of the most powerful settings where writers are given an opportunity to encounter readers. Although I find book tours very difficult because there is often too much contact within short amounts of time, they do allow writers to meet their public. These events are important because they provide one of the rare spaces in contemporary culture where people come together and mingle across race, class, and gender without having to pay a fee to do so. The bookstore reading remains one of the most democratic locations where ideas are exchanged in our society. Even if there is no question and answer between the writer and the public, the audience has the opportunity to chat with one another. This is significant precisely because there are not that many public spaces where ideas are exchanged without cost in our society. Nowadays, most bookstores allow the reading public to sit and really peruse a book so that someone who cannot afford to buy work still has an opportunity to look at the contents.

I wanted to write this essay as a gesture of gratitude to the many readers who have taken the time to share their thoughts about my work with me. We live, read, and/or write in an anti-intellectual society. Vast numbers of people are illiterate and do not know the pleasure of reading. It is easy for writers, especially dissident voices, to feel as though we write in isolation. When readers communicate with writers about our work, that sense of isolation is disrupted. I

would not have written so many books without the passion of readers, without their urging me to write more.

Writers should not dwell on the issue of audience. However, it is
essential for any writer who wants to speak to a general audience
without perpetuating structures of domination to write in a manner
that welcomes any reader. Writers do not need to worry about
whether our words can carry us across the boundaries of race, sex,
and class. Words invite us to transgress—to move beyond the world
of the ordinary. If that were not so the world of the book would have
no meaning. This does not mean that writers should not be vigilant
about the way we use words. Here the old truism "It's not what you
say but how you say it" holds. Irrespective of the subject matter,
whether it reflects a common experience or not, readers are capable
of great empathy. Writers must trust that readers are ready to
receive our words—to grapple with the strange and unfamiliar or to
know again what is already known in new ways.

the writer's true home

When I lived in a small town away from the world of big-time publishing, almost all my energies were concentrated on the vocation of writing. I did not have an agent. Then my books were all published by an alternative press. Since advances were not an issue (as the press did not offer them) I did not sit around fretting about how much money I would collect and when. While I thought about audiences (every writer wants readers), I can truthfully state that I did not spend much time thinking about whether my writing could be sold for lots of money. Then, I was clear about the life I wanted to lead: I wanted to live a simple life.

In my small town, it was and is easy to keep life simple. I had a daily routine. I would be awake early to meditate and exercise, then I would write. By afternoon, I would wander around town, ending up at the local bookstore. Later I would watch a movie and read. Nothing much interfered with this routine. Like many writers what I most lacked in this world full of the stillness and space for contemplation that is essential for thoughtful creative work was meaningful engaged conversation. A really great conversation can be such a stimulus to any writer who works with ideas. Of course in my town I have friends with whom I talk about all the important issues of life. It was just that I wanted the talk to go deeper, to extend itself like a high note from a soprano saxophone, extend itself in such a way as to remind the listener of the transcendent power of words and ideas.

My decision to move to a city was motivated by the desire for substantive conversation, especially for talk with other writers. I also wanted to expand the reading audience for my work. All my writing peers had agents. They assured me an agent would not only help me to sell my work for more money but that by doing this I would automatically acquire a larger audience. Younger black women writers who had not yet published books but who were way more sophisticated about the nature of publishing than myself urged me to find an agent and indeed shared their information. On my own I had contacted a black woman agent who had shown no interest in me or my work. I could not discern whether it was the feminist aspect of my work that made her deem it irrelevant and uninteresting, but she did not encourage me to send her manuscripts. Then a young black woman writer who had not yet published a book suggested I speak with her agent, who had just sold her proposed book for more than two hundred thousand dollars. This was an impressive sale.

For years I had naively believed that if authors were paid advances and the published manuscript did not sell we were required to pay the money back. Given this assumption I could not understand the reasons anyone wanted huge advances. It astonished me to discover that no one paid back advances when work did not sell; the publishing company simply writes off the unearned advance. Another younger black woman writer, Rebecca Walker, daughter of Alice Walker, encouraged me to talk with her mother's agent. All the agents I spoke with prior to meeting this agent had intently impressed upon my consciousness that black writers were the "in thing" and that they could really sell my work. One agent assured me that she could deliver enough money for me to buy that loft in Soho that I wanted. I did not doubt her words, for she was known for her six-figure advances. Yet the crass materialism that informed her ways of talking about writers and writing was alienating to me. And I could see why writers new to the very art and act of writing, eager to make money and a name for themselves, would not necessarily find anything disturbing about this approach.

It disturbed me because I was not accustomed to thinking of my writing as a commodity to be sold to the highest bidder, nor was I at all interested in creating a public persona that would be part of a marketing package. After all, I was the writer who had published books where I had religiously refused to use a picture of myself on the cover. I had rejected blurbs because I wanted the ideas in the work to be the selling feature. The ideas in my books did attract readers. While the alternative press did not give advances then or pay royalties on schedule, the books had sold. In my undergraduate creative-writing classes, I had learned from the published writers who taught these courses that few of us would ever make money from writing or become well known. The only reason I went to graduate school and acquired a Ph.D. in American literature was so that I could support myself as a writer. Everyone knew that academics writing books were lucky to find a publisher and a few readers. In those days no one that I knew saw writing as a way to make a living.

Twenty years later all that had changed. Writers were not only making a living from their work, they were receiving huge sums of money. At forty years old I moved to New York City hoping to change my fate as a writer. I dreamed of leaving my academic career since I was only well suited for teaching and not at all inclined to do administrative work. I chose a high-powered agent (the one recommended by Rebecca Walker) who was not crass in her approach, who was sincerely engaged with books and writers. Her style was low-key and nonintrusive. And most importantly she was interested in selling the work, not in shaping work so that it would be salable or in shaping salable writers. This pleased me because I wanted attention to be focused on the work, not on me. Most of my writing years had been spent in relative isolation. While my books were well known not that much was known about me.

When my agent auctioned my first book to a mainstream publisher she included in her packet photocopied statements that showed how well my other books had sold. At one point in the process she shared with me the feedback that she might not be able to get a large sum of money since the individuals in publishing she was trying to sell the work to were not familiar with the work. It did not matter to the world of mainstream publishing that the books I had published with an alternative were not only steadily selling but were being taught in almost every university in the United States; the fact remained that I was a "nobody" on the New York scene. These experiences were all lessons teaching me about publishing today. I learned that the young writers who received big bucks even though they had not yet sold any work were individuals whose names were "known" largely because they wrote for local newspapers and magazines. I was learning that it was more important to have a marketable name than to write a good book.

Most of my writing life I had shown no interest in writing for magazines. At times when I was working on a book of essays, if a magazine editor approached me I would agree to publish a piece, but I never wrote essays specifically for magazines. My experience with the publishing world in New York changed that. I began to write for newspapers and magazines so that my name would be out there—so that I would be a writer editors would recognize. I justified this shift in my own approach by telling myself that these actions were necessary for me to acquire a larger reading audience. On several occasions, encouraged by agent and editors, I passively submitted when my work was edited in ways that seemed to me to remove its provocative edge. I was encouraged to believe that these compromises would in the long run help to expand my audience. To some extent this strategy was helpful even though it was still the issues the works addressed that attracted readers as well. All the strategies I deployed to expand the audience for my books worked. My agent also acquired another contract for me with a substantial advance. Concurrently, media focus on black intellectuals also catapulted me into the public limelight, which brought greater attention to the work.

Suddenly, I was no longer a writer working in private. Whether I wanted it or not, the media created for me a public persona. Having a broader base to share ideas was the most exhilarating aspect of this newly acquired notoriety. It also created the opportunity for me to meet other thinkers and writers with whom I had longed to engage in conversation. More often than not the conversations about ideas and aesthetic concerns that I had imagined taking place did not happen. Usually, everyone was most interested in talking about the business of publishing, trading information or comparing notes. And high on everyone's list was the issue of how much money people were being paid for book deals. Like other writers who were for a long time ignorant of the way publishing works, I was amazed to learn that writers who had already received huge sums of money for books that did not sell well were still able to negotiate new and better contracts. I was told by folks working within the industry that it was simply because these individuals had "star" power, that everyone could know a book was lacking in literary merit but if the author's persona was strong enough to attract global attention that mattered more. It was difficult to make sense of it all when I was being told that my work could not attract huge sums because editors feared it would not sell. Of course the fact that my books have all sold well can be conveniently ignored since it is not fact that matters; connections and persona matter more.

As my awareness of the publishing interest intensified, I encountered extreme cynicism from editors young and old about the vocation of writing. Most folks seemed to have no interest in artistic visions or an author's relation to the craft of writing because the prevailing assumption was that any salable idea no matter how poorly thrown together could be shaped editorially into a viable commodity. From the moment I moved to New York I kept hearing from agents and editors that black writers were the "hot ticket." Rarely did anyone talk about particular authors or their work; instead they talked as if anything a black person wrote, no matter how uninteresting, could be marketed. A black woman visual artist shared with me that an editor called her to find out if she had considered writing a novel. She shared that she had nothing down on paper even though this was one of her fantasies. On the basis of sharing her ideas she was offered a contract. Her ability to write was not considered at all important. Hearing this I was reminded of the editor who told me that "it is actually better to work with writers who lack skill as they are more willing to allow their writing to be pushed in the right direction"—the right direction being always the one that will sell.

From the earliest years I spent in creative-writing classes at an elite university to my days as a professor of English at Yale, I found that my nonblack peers simply assumed black folks were not really serious about writing—or were rarely, if ever, great writers. The publishing industry seems to relish this assumption. It helps agents and editors to look at black writers and would-be writers as mere fodder for commodification. Words and bodies can be commodified in ways that do not reflect any concern with artistic vision and integrity. When young black writers who have not yet created a body of work, who may not even have a vision of what they hope to achieve in the writing, become more engaged with the process of making deals than fashioning words for the page their creativity is sorely diminished. If their primary concern is making money and not writing this diminishment will not have any serious impact. Yet some young writers who receive huge advances for work that then does not sell lose heart. They come away from this experience feeling as though they have failed when in fact the failure rests within the publishing industry.

Like every black writer who has spent most of his or her writing life away from the world of publishing, I found it disturbing to arrive on the contemporary scene only to find that there are way too few black folks in the industry. Beginning with agents and on to every sphere of the publishing process, within the industry workers are mainly white. This is especially the case among the major power brokers. An institution or industry may be peopled predominately by white individuals but if those individuals have divested of racism then whiteness in and of itself does not mean that their choices of what to read and publish will be shaped by racist biases. The same can be said of gender. Unfortunately race, sex, and class biases continue to shape not only what is published (which books are pushed by companies) but how work is received. Whenever I read periodicals devoted to reviewing books I am continually amazed that white male writers from privileged class backgrounds continue to have such hegemony of presence.

There are many black writers who believe that this situation will never change, that our work no matter how well written or important will never receive deserved regard and recognition within the existing structure. Certainly, it was disheartening to witness the biases informed by racism and sexism that surfaced when Toni Morrison won the Nobel Prize. While this deserved recognition should have been a marker of change, for critics intent on maintaining the status quo it became an occasion for vilification. Suddenly critics who had never felt the need to comment on the merits of Morrison's work were seeking to discredit it. Her work was subjected to a type of mean-spirited criticism that was unlike that any other Nobel Prize–winning author had received. Sexist and racist biases were at the heart of all the trashing that denounced Morrison's writing. There was no meaningful critique offered. Serious writing by black authors is always subjected to harsher critique than more frivolous literary contributions.

The black writer who does not even try to feign interest in the craft of writing is more likely to be well received than anyone of us who embraces a vision of excellence. It is quite noticeable that anytime a young black writer receives a lot of money for a book deal this becomes a topic for the press to focus on. Embedded in such discussion is the assumption that some outrageously unfair practice of affirmative action is taking place where the minorities are receiving more than they deserve. In actuality, for every undeserving mediocre black writer, young or old, receiving a substantial book deal there are large numbers of equally undeserving mediocre white writers receiving deals as good or better. Publishers will put money behind a book by a black writer only after they have proven their sales potential. Unfortunately, good books by black writers often receive no serious attention financial or otherwise because they do not interest a fast-food, commodity-driven publishing industry. It is tragically ironic that an industry that for so long believed that black audiences did not constitute a market for books now accepts that this assumption was wrong even as it then markets to that newly acknowledged audience so much work that is simply on the level of substandard housing.

Unscrupulous agents and editors do their part to persuade black writers (along with writers from all other groups) that it is better to focus on making money than to strive for writing excellence. Now that many of the students that I have taught at Yale and Oberlin work in the publishing industry, I hear from them firsthand accounts of rewriting material that comes to them hastily and poorly written. Young writers of all races whom I encounter see issues of ethics and integrity as concerns of the naive, of those who a young agent suggested to me are just not "hungry enough." When I came to New York I believed that it would be possible to garner greater financial reward for work well done, acquire a larger audience for my work, and maintain my integrity as a writer. Experience has confirmed that all this is possible.

It takes critical vigilance not to be swept away by all the forces of materialist greed that encourage any writer eager to be more successful to dispense with integrity in the interest of making the big deals. Writer Jeanette Winterson encourages authors to hold to that integrity in *Art {Objects}*: "Integrity is the true writer's determination not to buckle under market forces, not to strangle her own voice for the sake of a public who prefers its words in whispers. The pressures on young writers to produce to order and to produce more of the same, if they have had a success, is now at overload, and the media act viciously in either ignoring or pillorying any voice that is not their kind of journalese. A writer needs to be unswayed by praise or blame and skeptical of the easy friendships and sudden enmities offered by the industry in which she now has to work."

Quiet as it is kept there are many writers who simply want to have the freedom to work on pursuing writing as a vocation without having to endlessly hustle for money or work at steady jobs all the time. Having enough to live on as a writer does not mean that one needs huge advances. Yet there is tremendous pressure for every writer to go for the highest remuneration possible as though this gesture proves that one is really serious or has really made it. When I have shared with agents and editors that I am wary of huge advances that bring with them lots of demands on one's time as I seek to protect both writing time and time spent in contemplation and preparation for writing, they have dismissed these concerns as unimportant.

Writers who do not have fantasies of making the big deals, of acquiring major fortune or fame from work need to be acknowledged if for no other reason than that younger writers can see that it is possible to be content as a writer doing one's work and receiving a measure of recognition. Winterson's insistence that we stay focused on work resonates with me: "The writer should refuse all definitions; of herself, and of her work, and remember that whether her work sells or whether it doesn't, whether it is loved or it is not, it is the same piece of work. Reaction cannot alter what is written. And what is written is the writer's true home." When one succeeds with writing cynical observers often assume that this is a sign that one is not primarily devoted to work. In my case, when critics wrote about my "success" they never mentioned the many years I wrote books in relative isolation, with no advances, without even regular royalty payments when the work did sell well. For me the heartbeat of it all has been and continues to be writing—not publishing, not selling.

I know the value of a life informed by devotion to the art and craft of writing. That is the life I lived before coming to reside in a city where the impact of the publishing industry is so keenly felt in everyday life. Even when I sit at home in my flat writing, the buzzer may ring and a messenger will come to my door bringing me news from the industry, a request, a new book, etc. Now and then I relish this immediacy, but at other times it serves as a constant reminder that it's about business, not books. The pleasure I received from the hard work of writing was much greater when I lived away from the workings of this industry. While I have no regrets about the time I have spent in the city learning more about publishing, pushing my own work so that I now have both a larger audience and greater opportunity for financial reward, I have already reclaimed a more reclusive space where the power and passion of writing, simply writing, prevails. In that space I do not obsess about audiences, advances, or critical reviews, I just give my all to the work at hand.

To write with too much of a mind for business changes the nature and spirit of the words that come together on the page. Hedonistic materialism has the power to alter brilliant insights no matter how pure the original vision. Years ago when I first began publishing with South End Press the collective was deeply committed to accepting work that they believed deserved a hearing, especially writing that the mainstream publishing industry had turned away. Had material reward been their sole concern my work and that of many other writers might not have received the initial affirmation that served as a foundation we could build upon. After the success both critical and financial of my first book, I could have left the world of alternative publishing to try and make it in the mainstream. I stayed with alternatives for a long time to nurture and sustain my own belief that desire for material reward should never be greater than the desire to create writing that is solid, insightful, honest—writing that can move the reader, give them an experience of words, cultivated by tender devotion to the art and craft of writing.

black women writing

creating more space

To many people, black women writers are everywhere—on the cover of *Newsweek*, the *New York Times Magazine*, on talk shows, on speaking circuits. Just the other day I was in a bookstore and the clerk who took my money for Paule Marshall's novel *Praisesong for the Widow* told me if I intend to write a novel, this is the time—that "they" are looking for black women writers. "They" are the publishers and they are supposedly looking for us because our work is a new commodity. The invisible "they" who control publishing may have only recently fully realized that there is a market for fiction written by black women, but it does not necessarily follow that they are actively seeking to find more material by black women; that black women are writing more than ever before; or that it is any easier for unknown black women writers to find ways to publish their work. It is more likely that those black women writers who have been writing unnoticed for some time, who have already found a way to get their foot in the door or have managed to open it wider have managed to enter and can now find publishers for their work.

Publication of their work reminds me and many black women writers/readers that our voices can be heard, that if we create, there is "hope" that our work will one day be published. I am always excited when I hear that another black woman writer has published (fiction or any other genre), especially if she is new and unknown. The more of us there are entering the publishing world the more likely we will continue writing. Yet we are not entering the publishing world in large numbers. Every time someone comments on the "tremendous" attention black women writers are receiving, how easy it is for us to find publishers, how many of us there are, I stop and count, make lists, sit in groups of black women and try to come up with new names. What we've noticed is that the number of visible, published black women writers of fiction is not large. Anyone who teaches courses on black women's fiction knows how difficult it is to find the works of black women (they go out of print rapidly, do not get reprinted, or if reprinted come out in editions that are so expensive that students can rarely afford to buy them for their personal libraries and certainly cannot teach them in classes where many books must be purchased). The reprinted edition of Gwendolyn Brooks's *Maud Martha* (first published in 1953) is one example. It is however better to have expensive reprints rather than no reprints. Books like Ann Petry's *The Street*, Jessie Fauset's *Plum Bun*, Frances Harper's *Iola Leroy*, Kristin Hunter's *The Survivors* and *The Lakestown Rebellion* are often not available. Yet all of these black women writers were or are well known and their works were or are widely read.

I assume that publishing quotas exist that determine the number of black women who will publish books of fiction yearly. Such quotas are not consciously negotiated and decided upon but are the outcomes of institutionalized racism, sexism, and classism. These systems of domination operate in such a way as to ensure that only a very few fiction books by black women will be published at any given time. This has many negative implications for black women writers, those who are published and those who have yet to be published. Published black women writers, even those who are famous, are well aware that their successes do not ensure that their books will be on bookstore shelves years from now. They know that the spirit of new commodity faddism that stimulates much of the current interest in black women's writing can dissipate. It is likely that these writers know that they must "strike while the iron is hot" and this knowledge produces the sense that they cannot always wait for inspiration, cannot linger too long between the publication of one book and the writing of another. They are often compelled to spread themselves thin—teaching, writing, giving talks in the interest of making a living but also in the interest of promoting awareness of the existence and significance of their work. These pressures, whether imposed or chosen, will necessarily affect the writer's work.

Black women writers who are not published, who are still nurturing and developing their skills often find it difficult to maintain the sense that what they have to say is important, especially if they are not in an environment where their commitment to writing is encouraged and affirmed. They must also struggle with the demands of surviving economically while writing. The difficulty of this process for black women has changed little through the years. For every one black woman writer that manages to be published, hundreds if not thousands cease writing because they cannot withstand the pressures, cannot sustain the effort without affirmation, or because they fear that to risk everything in pursuit of one's creative work seems foolish because so few will make it in the end.

Often new writers find that college creative-writing courses provide a positive atmosphere wherein one's work will be read, critiqued, affirmed. Black women attending universities could and do find in such courses a place to strengthen creative writing skills. However, black students are rarely present in these courses at campuses where students are predominantly white. At some campuses where students are predominantly black there is often little or no interest in creative writing. Young black women recognize the precariousness of our collective economic lot (increased unemployment, poverty, etc.) and tend to look for those courses that strengthen their ability to succeed in careers. The promising young black woman writer who must work to provide or help provide for herself and family often cannot find the energy or time to concentrate on and develop her writing. Often black women in professions (teachers, doctors, lawyers, etc.) who are also writers find that the demands of their jobs often leave little room for the cultivation of creative work.

Few black women have imagined that they can make a living writing. I was thirteen when I decided that I wanted to be a writer. At that time I was primarily writing poetry and I realized that I would not be able to make a living with writing. I chose to study literature because I thought it would lead to a profession compatible with writing. When poetry was my primary concern I was fascinated by the work lives of poets who had professions but wrote extensively. Many of these poets were men—Langston Hughes, Wallace Stevens, William Carlos Williams. When I read about their lives I did not reflect on the supportive role women played in the lives of heterosexual male writers, who were probably not coping with domestic chores or raising children while working in professional jobs and writing (their female companions probably attended to these matters). Rare is the woman writer of any race who is free (from domestic chores or caring for others—children, parents, companions) to focus solely on her writing. I know of few black women writers who have been able to concentrate solely on their development as writers without working other jobs at the same time.

In retrospect I can see that I was always trying to attend college, hold part-time jobs, and make a space for writing, as well as taking care of domestic matters. It has become clear to me that I was most free to develop as a writer/poet when I was home with my parents and they were providing economic support, with mama doing the majority of domestic chores and all the cooking. This was the time in my life when I had time to read, study, and write. They and my siblings were also continually affirming my creativity, urging me to develop my talent (after I did my small number of assigned chores). I often heard from them and other folk in the community that talent was a gift from God, and was not to be taken lightly but nourished, developed, or it would be taken away. While I no longer hear this message literally—that the ability to write will be taken away—I do see that the more I write the easier and more joyous a labor it becomes. The less I write the harder it is for me to write and the more it appears to be so arduous a task that I seek to avoid it. I think if any would-be writer avoids writing long enough then they are likely to "lose" the desire, the ability, the power to create.

One must write and one must have time to write. Having time to write, time to wait through silences, time to go to the pen and paper or typewriter when the breakthrough finally comes, affects the type of work that is written. When I read contemporary black women's fiction I see much similarity in choices of subject matter, geographical location, use of language, character formation, and style. There could be many reasons for such similarities. On the one hand, there is the reality of the social status black women share, which has been shaped by the impact of sexism and racism on our lives and shared cultural and ethic experiences. On the other hand, there is the possibility that many of us pattern work after the fiction of those writers who have been published and are able to earn a living as writers. There is also the possibility that a certain type of writing (the linear narrative story) may be easier to write because it is more acceptable to the reading public than experimental works, especially those that would not focus on themes of black experience or tell a story in a more conventional way. These restrictions apply to many groups of writers in our society. It is important that there be diversity in the types of fiction black women produce and that varied types of writing by black women receive attention and be published. There should not be a stereotyped image of a black woman writer or a preconceived assumption about the type of fiction she will produce.

It must not be assumed that the successes of contemporary black women writers like Toni Morrison, Alice Walker, Paule Marshall, Toni Cade Bambara, Ntozake Shange, and others indicate that a new day has arrived for a majority or even a substantial minority of black women writers. Their individual successes and continued creative development are crucial components of what should be an overall artistic movement to encourage and support writing by black women. Such a movement could take many forms. On a very basic level it can begin with communities stressing the importance of young black children acquiring reading and writing skills and developing along with those skills a positive attitude toward writing. Many of us learned reading and writing but disliked or hated writing. Throughout my twenty years of teaching at a number of universities I have witnessed the terror and anguish many students feel about writing. Many acknowledge that their hatred and fear of writing surfaced in grade school and gathered momentum through high school, reaching a paralyzing peak in the college years.

An intense effort to create and sustain interest in writing must take place in schools and communities. Entering writing competitions should be encouraged by parents, teachers, and friends for young writers. Black women and other people who are interested in the future development of black writers should establish more writing competitions where prizes could be as low as twenty-five dollars to stimulate interest in writing. There should be grant programs for newly published but not yet successful black women writers so that we can have a summer or a year to concentrate solely on our work. Though programs exist that fund writers (like the National Endowment for the Humanities), only the occasional lucky black woman writer receives one of these grants. Often the same few writers receive a number of grants from different sources. While this is good for the individual, it does not increase the number of black women writers receiving aid. Money could be given to a number of universities to sponsor individual black women as part of creative-writing programs.

It seems easier for black women writers to receive monetary support of one kind or another, grants, teaching positions, and talks after they have struggled in isolation and achieved success. Yet only a few black women writers make it in this way. It took me seven years to finish the writing of *Ain't I a Woman: Black Women and Feminism* in part because I did extensive research before writing but also because every avenue I turned toward seeking monetary support failed. I would write after working my eight hours a day at the phone company or after other jobs. When the book was completed almost six years before it was published I sent it off to a number of publishers who rejected it. Without the support of my companion, who helped both financially and emotionally (affirming me as a writer), it would have been impossible to continue. I hear this same story from other black women who know firsthand, as I do, how devastating working in isolation can be. On several occasions I contacted established black women writers seeking acceptance, advice, and critiques but got little response. However, Alice Walker was one person who told me that she was very busy but would take time to read the manuscript if she could. I did not send it to her because I felt that I was imposing, perhaps taking her attention away from her work. Also I think the other black women writers I approached were constantly asked to respond, to give support and advice to younger writers and there is a point when one must say no if you are overextended.

Black women need not be the only group who give support and affirmation to aspiring black female writers. A teacher, friend, or colleague can provide the encouragement and affirmation that fosters and promotes work. When I first met Gloria Naylor, author of the novel *The Women of Brewster Place*, I asked her how she had found a publisher. Gloria was a student at Yale working on an M.A. focusing on creative writing. She found support and affirmation for her work in this academic environment. It was with the help of a friend that she was able to find an editor to read her novel and consider it for publication. Having people around who affirm one during the writing process is as vital to the aspiring writer as finding someone to publish one's work.

When I was an undergraduate taking creative-writing courses, I remember a black male poet advising me not to worry about publication but to focus on writing, then when I had produced a body of work to worry about finding a publisher. This bit of advice has been very useful over the years, reminding me that the primary emphasis for the aspiring writer has to be initially on the production of work. I find in teaching creative-writing classes that aspiring writers are often so desperate for the affirmation that comes with publication that they are not interested in rewriting, or putting away a piece for a time and coming back to it. After *Ain't I a Woman* was rejected I spent almost nine months away from the work before I took the box down from its hiding place in the closet and began massive rewriting. Like Gloria Naylor, I learned from a friend who had seen their ad in a Bay Area women's newspaper that South End Press was seeking books on feminism and race. In retrospect, despite the pain I suffered when the manuscript was continually rejected, I can see now that it was not ready for publication at that time. I now consider it fortunate that no one accepted it then. I have completed many books that focus on feminist and cultural issues, one poetry manuscript, one dissertation, two novels in manuscript, and yet I still confront daily the difficulty of providing for myself economically while seeking to grow and develop as a writer.

When I told Chinosole, a black woman friend and fellow writer-scholar, about this essay, she commented that it is amazing how much writing we black women can produce even when we are worried sick about finances and job pressures. It is my hope that the current interest in works of a few black women writers will lead to the recognition of the need to encourage and promote such writing—not just the work of famous black women but the work of unknown, struggling, aspiring writers who need to know that their creative work is important, that it deserves their concentrated attention, and that it need not be abandoned.

zora neale hurston

a subversive reading

Although much is written about Zora Neale Hurston's life, her flamboyant personality, there is little information about her engagement with books. What writers did she read and like? Whose work influenced her writing? Robert Hemenway's biography mentions only that

> Zora learned to read before school age, and her quickness set her apart. Of all the school's students it was the fifth grader Zora Hurston who so impressed two visiting Yankee ladies that they were moved to send her a box of books. Suddenly her single-volume library, the family's Bible, was augmented by Grimm's fairy tales, Greek and Roman myths, Norse legends, Kipling, and Robert Louis Stevenson.

Like Hurston, diverse books I could call my own first came into my childhood as gifts—a retired black schoolteacher was cleaning out her house and throwing away shoeboxes filled with tiny books in leather. They were the "classics" of white Western literature. From among these writers I chose one whose work influenced me, Emily Dickinson.

At thirteen, I knew I wanted to write. Confident that this was my destiny, at sixteen I read Virginia Woolf's *A Room of One's Own* and chose another guide. She was the sister-informant, sharing the secrets of what it would mean to be a woman and a writer, telling me what I would need. I never thought of Dickinson or Woolf as "white women." They entered the segregated world of my growing up as writers, and most importantly as women writers. Later I would learn the distance separating their experience from my own, the politics of race, sex, and class—still their work spoke to me. However, it was the discovery of black writers in general, and black women writers in particular, that fully affirmed that I could indeed become a writer, that it was vital and necessary to draw upon the experience of black culture and black life for inspiration and imaginative direction. Zora Neale Hurston became the representative mentor for me. Her background was similar to my own (rural, southern, religious, lacking in material privilege) and I was profoundly impressed by her commitment to writing, to breaking through silences, and her willingness to experiment with form and content.

Like many readers I have often thought *Their Eyes Were Watching God* most fascinating because of the way it challenges conventional sexist notions of woman's role in marriage and romantic love, insisting on the importance of female self-actualization. I, too, have celebrated Hurston's fictional portrait of love between a black woman and man. Critical attention has necessarily focused on these aspects of the novel, so intensely however that readers are inclined to overlook Hurston's concern with the construction of "female imagination" and the formation of a critical space where woman's creativity can be nurtured and sustained. These concerns radically inform the structure of *Their Eyes Were Watching God* and its narrative direction. They can be fully addressed only if readers no longer centralize Janie's relationships with men. Strategically, the focus on romance is a device Hurston uses to engage readers while subtly interjecting a subversive narrative.

Hurston's passion for the folktale that captivates audiences by sharing a story cast in terms that appear familiar, coupled with her sense that stories were most interesting when lies masked truth, greatly influenced her writing style. Barbara Johnson comments on this strategy:

> If, as Hurston often implies, the essence of telling "lies" is the art of conforming a narrative to existing structures of address while gaining the upper hand, then Hurston's very ability to fool us into thinking we have been fooled—is itself the only effective way of conveying the rhetoric of the "lie."

Much of Hurston's magic and power as a writer centers on her incredible ability to manipulate multiple plots in a single narrative. Her insistence on playful subterfuge is often missed by readers of *Their Eyes Were Watching God* who see the novel as conventional linear narrative weakened by textual gaps.

Discussing the work of nineteenth-century white women writers, Eva Figes reminds readers in her chapter on "The Suppressed Self" that it was "not remotely possible for women to express themselves through fiction in terms of full individuation, because they were not free." She emphasizes that internal and external constraints ensured that woman's subjective voice would be "expressed with a certain degree of disguise and subterfuge." These comments hold true for black women's writing in the early twentieth century.

Structural ambiguity is not a failing in Hurston's work, it is a tactic, leading the unsuspecting reader astray. Within traditional African-American folk culture, telling a story to a listener who perpetually misses the point was seen as an indication that they were not meant to "hear" the message. They could enjoy the story without understanding it. One constructs a tale so that it appears to address everyone even though it speaks in its deepest structure to a select few. Without a doubt, Hurston intended *Their Eyes Were Watching God* to be an appealing story, one that would sell to a wide audience. To enhance the likelihood of such appeal she exploits many conventional aspects of romantic fiction. Yet she was not writing a romance. There are many plots and much social commentary in *Their Eyes Were Watching God*. One very moving story is the romance of Janie and Tea Cake. Just as everyone comes to the courtroom to hear Janie tell her story (the narrator comments, "Who was it didn't know about the love between Tea Cake and Janie"), it is this story more so than any other told in the novel that continues to have appeal—it speaks to everyone.

Critics talk about the love between Janie and Tea Cake as the catalyst for her self-actualization, using the metaphor of her "coming to voice"—becoming a storyteller—as a sign of female empowerment. Consistently read as a novel that celebrates Janie's finding a voice, readers are nevertheless disturbed by the concrete fictive circumstance that frames Janie's autonomous identity as the novel closes. Hortense Spillers' critique implies that Hurston's ending betrays the characterization of Janie as self-actualized. Reading the ending as a "eulogy for the living," she suggests that "Janie has been 'buried' along with Tea Cake." In an even more suspicious reading, one that goes against the grain, Mary Helen Washington asserts that the novel "represents women's exclusion from power, particularly from the power of oral speech." Approaching the novel primarily through a comparative lens where Janie's status is viewed in contrast to that of men or contemporary feminist standards, these readings simplify Hurston's vision. Spillers focuses on the persistence of Tea Cake's presence, even after his death, and Washington calls attention to the few times Janie actually "speaks."

They read gaps in the novel as lacks, representing Hurston's failed or distorted insight. These gaps can be viewed as narrative clues underscoring the extent to which Hurston's critical project was not simply to create a female hero who resists sexist oppression, asserting autonomy, selfhood. When she stops speaking through the text to a mass audience engaged in empathic identification with Janie's effort to resolve her quest for love and selfhood, Hurston speaks to her select few. Then the novel is more a fictive manifesto on the subject of gender roles as they influence and affect the construction of the female imagination. It echoes and extends the commentary Woolf begins in *A Room of One's Own*, centralizing the plight of underclass black women who might wish to develop their creative talent.

Janie's quest for selfhood ends in her return to a space where she can be solitary, critically reflective, where she can "tell her story." Significantly, she returns economically self-sufficient—the material conditions that Woolf charges are necessary for any woman desiring to write. Just as Woolf delivers her important comments on female creativity to an audience of women, Janie tells her story to a black woman, Pheoby, inviting her to share the tale with others. Expressing confidence in Pheoby's ability to convey the truth of her experience, Janie offers a provocative metaphor for sisterhood, declaring, "Mah tongue is in mah friend's mouf." Much of the language describing their friendship is romantic—intimate and familiar. As storyteller and listener they complement each other. A similar complementarity exists between Janie and the third-person narrator who intervenes and shares the telling of Janie's story.

Unlike the conventional third-person narrator who assumes a privileged distance from the story, Hurston's narrator is engaged, familiar, and intimate. The tone the narrator uses is akin to Janie's even though it is a more sophisticated voice. Some critics see Hurston's use of third-person narration as a gesture that undermines the development of Janie's voice. Mary Helen Washington assumes that "Hurston was indeed ambivalent about giving a powerful voice to a woman like Janie who is already in rebellion against male authority and against the role prescribed for women in a male-dominated setting." Had the story been told in Janie's fictive patois there would have been little or no space for the inclusion of a wide range of folklore and folk wisdom (much of which surfaces in dialogues between characters Janie would not have been in a position to hear). Hurston's skillful repression of Janie's voice never jeopardizes its significance. Even though readers do not hear her voice in the courtroom scene, we learn that she moved her audience, that she achieved the desired effect. Third-person narration does not deflect attention away from that achievement, or Hurston's didactic insistence that women must come to voice to be fully self-empowered. If Hurston was ambivalent, her concern may have been that the novel not be viewed as a fictive sociology of black folklife. Though she wanted to celebrate folk experience in her writing, she wanted readers to recognize that her novel was a carefully constructed imaginative work. Third-person narration calls attention to Hurston's authorial voice, highlighting the importance of writing.

Zora Neale Hurston could easily have become a renowned oral storyteller; she chose writing. *Their Eyes Were Watching God* celebrates storytelling as imaginative work that can serve as the foundation for the development of a written story. It is this fictive art form (oral storytelling in the African-American folk tradition) that most influenced Hurston's work. Hence the importance of her fictive opposition to black male domination, which precludes female participation in oral storytelling. This critique implies that denying black women access to a mode of artistic expression that is so fundamental a ritual of daily life is an exclusionary practice that eliminates any possibility that females can develop their imaginative skills.

Suppression of female imagination does not begin in *Their Eyes Were Watching God* with male domination. Hurston links the realm of fantasy and imagination to the experience of eros (desire) and sexual awakening. At sixteen Janie's ecological communion with a pollinating pear tree stirs her senses, simultaneously stimulating a desire for knowledge. Intuitively experiencing an erotic metaphysic wherein she witnesses the unity of all life, Janie confronts her ignorance, the absence of an ontological framework that could serve as a basis for the construction of autonomous self and identity. Acknowledging her longing to "struggle with life" she is eager to follow intuition, to become a seeker on the path of self-realization. These longings and her unrepressed imagination are stifled by her grandmother, whose vision of life has been overtly determined by racist and sexist politics of domination. Using a popular folktale (one Hurston did not create) Janie's grandmother explains the way the convergence of race, class, and gender domination shape the social circumstance of black women. A political commentary that concludes with the statement "De nigger woman is de mule uh de world." Materialist to her core, Janie's grandmother confronts the harsh reality of white supremacist capitalist patriarchy and strategically defines the terms of her survival, working within the existing structure. It is this nonoppositional legacy she shares with Janie, forcing her to adopt a similar survival strategy. Her imaginative exploration of the meaning of existence and her sexuality are all suppressed in the interest of material survival.

Unable to envision new paradigms for black womanhood, Janie conforms. Her marriage to a "good provider" ensures material survival even as it requires sexual and emotional repression. Yet Janie's erotic imagination is never completely submerged. Throughout the novel Hurston toys with the idea that eros can be a catalyst for self-discovery and transformation, that repression of this inner power leads to acquiescence, submission, domination. It is the convergence of power and desire that informs Janie's relationships to men. Given her race, class, and gender it is only through an involvement with a male that she can hope to change her circumstance. Hurston assumes that it is a natural outcome of patriarchal socialization that female imagination is most expressed initially within the realm of romantic fantasy. She evokes the "feminine ideal" only to show how it leads to the subjugation and subordination of the "desired" female. Janie is never completely taken in or corrupted by idealized notions of femininity. Though she outwardly conforms, inwardly she resists. Hurston portrays this contradiction sympathetically, though she is more scathing in her fictive social commentary on masculinity.

Men, Hurston suggests, are psychologically unable to be existentially self-reflective about masculinity. In *Their Eyes Were Watching God*, masculinity is seldom celebrated and often mocked. Hurston's focus on Janie's men is not male-identified, for she exposes and unmasks. Again, there are correlations between her strategy and the literary tactics Woolf employs in *A Room of One's Own*. In both works the characterization of men is double-edged and ironic. Hurston's portrait of Joe Starks is initially flattering, becoming progressively negative as his character unfolds. Despite social superiority, men in *Their Eyes Were Watching God* look good from afar; close-up their flaws and failings surface. They are preoccupied with representation, obsessed with appearances. Janie hardly notices her long hair and never focuses on physical beauty. She is attracted to men who behave in a manner that appeals. Ultimately, Hurston's fictional portrayals suggest that men lack substance.

All of Janie's loves—Logan Killicks, Joe Starks, and Tea Cake—are insanely egotistical. Each man suffers because he is unable to make full empathic connection with the world and people around him. On his deathbed, Joe is confronted with Janie's critical assessment of this failing. She tells him, "You was so busy worshippin' de works of yo' own hands, and cuffin' folks around in their minds till you didn't see uh whole heap up things yuh could have." Tea Cake's egotism leads him to ignore the signs and warnings that indicate a hurricane is coming. Risking his life and Janie's, he places himself above God and nature. A similar concern with image and masculine ego is evoked in the scene where Tea Cake hits Janie to prove to other men that she is "his" woman.

Feminist readers are usually disturbed by what appears to be Hurston's uncritical acceptance of male physical violence against women, overlooking the way in which the novel portrays violence as an integral part of the black folklife. The first person who slaps Janie is her grandmother. Tea Cake and Janie first struggle physically when she attacks him. Significantly, in the passage describing this conflict initial emphasis is placed on Tea Cake's efforts to talk with Janie. Her response is to "cut him short with a blow." Although their fighting ends in lovemaking, this is not a scenario advocating physical abuse of women—Janie is not represented as a victim of domination. Tea Cake restrains her to "keep her from going too far," suggesting she has the power to hurt him. Hurston was quite familiar with "shoot and cut" relationships where black women physically attacked and killed black men. She did not see black women within the communities of her growing up as passive victims of male abuse. Her uncritical acceptance of violence as a "natural" outcome of conflict should form the basis of feminist critique. There is a distinctly different tone in the novel when Hurston portrays Joe Starks's slapping Janie to maintain coercive male domination and Tea Cake's slaps. Starks's brutality is underscored. Tea Cake appears vulnerable, pathetic, and ridiculous. Hurston is critical of the circumstances and reasons why men are violent towards women. She calls attention to the way in which male notions of female inferiority must be continually reaffirmed by active aggression, thereby challenging notions of innate difference that would support the claim of male superiority.

Indeed, Hurston's characterizations of males and females often suggest that women are possibly the superior gender. Janie intervenes in male conversation to challenge the notion of male superiority. Claiming to be on intimate terms with God (who is constantly evoked as a power stronger than men), she asserts, "He tole me how surprised He was 'bout y'all turning out so smart after Him makin' yuh different." Divine presence magnified in nature is evoked by Hurston as part of her questioning of sexist defined roles. Using her fiction to denounce expressions of masculinity associated with coercive domination, she challenges the accepted belief that the male who is best able to provide material possessions is the most desirable companion. New paradigms for heterosexual bonding are suggested via the characterization of Tea Cake, in many ways an antimasculinist man with no desire to dominate others. Even though he has sexist attitudes, they are not the basis of his relationship with Janie. From the onset of their romantic bonding, Tea Cake introduces a model of heterosexual bonding based on reciprocity and mutuality. Susan Willis identifies the subversive nature of their relationship:

> Since possession and objectification do not define the dynamic of their union, Tea Cake and Janie are free to devote their energy and attention to maintaining reciprocity. When, at their first meeting, Tea Cake teaches Janie to play checkers, he sets the terms of their relationship in which all endeavor will be defined as sport and shared equality. Heterosexuality is neither a basis for power nor a reason for submission, but a mode in which a man and a woman might equally participate.

Tea Cake's alternative masculinity is linked to a repudiation of materialist values. Sustaining a nonexploitative relationship to nature, radical disengagement from a market economy, he is not alienated from a realm of expressive feelings and emotions, usually associated with children and women. Tea Cake values "play." He is able to express a wide range of emotions, to be empathic. Sharing his intuitive trust in the power of feelings and his belief that the desire to experience pleasure can be the organizing principle of daily life, he is able to help Janie recover the "feeling" self she has long repressed.

Through a shared eros, Janie reconnects with the passionate part of her being experienced in her adolescence. Through this reconnection she is able to heal her wounded psyche—to be born again. Recognizing the gift Tea Cake has given her, she affirms their bonding as they face the possibility of death: "If you kin see de light at daybreak, you don't keer if you die at dusk. It's so many people never see de light at all. Ah uz fumblin' round and God opened de door." More than an affirmation of her love for Tea Cake, this statement reveals Janie's belief in a divine force made manifest in human relations. The "light" here is not romantic love, it is spiritual awareness—vision, insight. Experiencing mutual romantic love has been a means for Janie to know divine love, to return to that erotic metaphysic expressed in her girlhood. Connecting with Tea Cake, she experiences anew the unity of all life. Returning to an uncorrupted natural environment—"the muck"—she learns to live in harmony with nature, with a multiethnic diverse community of people. In this world of unrepressed emotions she learns to sing and dance, to tell stories. Tea Cake nurtures Janie's growth, assuming a maternal role, yet another aspect of his alternative masculinity.

Hurston does not sustain the portrait of Tea Cake as symbol of oppositional, reconstructed, potentially feminist masculinity. His radical transgression of gender norms is undermined by sexist attitudes and behavior surfacing whenever he feels jealousy. During these times Tea Cake is obsessed by the desire to show others that he "possesses" Janie. Just as jealousy prompts his slapping her, it leads him to attack her when he is sick. After Tea Cake battles the mad dog, he completely reverts to a sexist masculine posture. Confiding in Janie the belief that his rescue of her affirms his masculinity, he asserts: "Ah want yuh tuh know it's uh man heah." Just as Janie has been a divided soul, passively submitting to sexist, defined female roles while alternately rebelling against those roles, Tea Cake both embraces and rejects aspects of traditional masculinity. His inability to disengage fully from sexist norms undermines the transformative power of feminist aspects of their heterosexual bonding. Attacking Janie, Tea Cake employs violent rhetoric similar to the verbal assaults of Janie's previous husbands, Logan Killicks and Joe Starks. Commanding her to "answer me when ah speak," Tea Cake assumes a dominating, threatening stance.

Ironically, Janie can effectively oppose the reinscription of a life-threatening male domination by using skills Tea Cake helped her to acquire. Their life-and-death confrontation is the ultimate test of her newly found self-regard. If she had become a whole person through loving and sharing life with Tea Cake, a person capable of autonomous individuation, she must shatter the illusion that "Tea Cake wouldn't hurt her"—facing reality. Acknowledging conflicting identities, the courageous self within "fighting for its life" and the "sacrificing self," Janie confidently chooses. No longer victimized by passivity and fearful inability to exercise autonomous resistance in the face of male domination, she reveals a decisive mindset. It is this climactic moment in the novel more so than any act of storytelling that indicates that Janie has constructed an autonomous self.

Janie's killing of Tea Cake subverts traditional notions of romantic love, which encourage female masochism; she is not willing to die for love. Earlier in the novel Janie has called attention to distortions and perversions in relationships enacted in the name of love, sharing her insight that "most humans didn't love one another." Hurston offers a different version of romantic love, one that repudiates female masochism. Though the two lovers initially experience a temporary loss of ego boundaries—Janie describes her feelings as "a self-crushing love" and Tea Cake expresses the depth of his surrender by declaring that she has "got de keys tuh de kingdom"—mutual growth and sharing leads to enhanced individuation. Despite Tea Cake's jealous fear that he will lose Janie, he encourages her to be self-sufficient. Though longing to assume the role of protector, he understands that she must learn to protect herself. At times both lovers don the mantle of androgyny, displaying characteristics commonly associated with the opposite sex. In an uncorrupted world of gender relations, Tea Cake can be a nurturer, can express vulnerability and fear; Janie can work and shoot like a man, she can even dress like a man. Through most of the novel, Janie's long hair is her distinguishing feature, the mark of her idealized femininity. On the muck it is no longer an important signifier. Their androgyny is represented as a utopian ideal.

A central idea in Woolf's *A Room of One's Own* is the assertion that great writing is created by an androgynous mind, that women and men must be able to transcend limited sex roles if the imagination, the source of a writer's power, is to have full expressive range. Woolf emphasizes that writers must be able to travel, to fully explore and experience life, stressing the way the female imagination suffers because women lack complete freedom of movement. In *Their Eyes Were Watching God* Janie longs to travel, to move freely. Her passionate desire to "journey to the horizon," to transcend boundaries, to be an adventurer is a repudiation of the traditional female role. Hurston's fictive characterization of the ease with which Janie flaunts convention, leaving marriage and comfortable material circumstances, having a love affair with a younger man, were daring authorial gestures for her time. Sensibly, Hurston does not suggest that Janie can wander alone; that would have given the novel less credibility. Witnessing Janie's various attempts to conform to societal norms, the containment and repression of her passionate adventurous nature, readers in the 1930s could sympathize with her plight and applaud her rebellion.

Hurston seizes every opportunity to reiterate the conviction that transgressive behavior that promotes and encourages self-exploration is essential for the development of an artistic sensibility. Critically reflecting about her past when Joe Starks dies, Janie laments the loss of intense creative impulses. Recalling her intuitive awareness of the importance of creativity in girlhood, she remembers thinking "she had found a jewel down inside herself." Then Janie saw herself as gifted. Falling in love with another gifted person, Tea Cake, she regains the power to imagine, to dream, to create. Bohemian in style, Tea Cake is both musician and composer. Art is an integral part of daily life, never separate or fetishized. Burying him with a new guitar, Janie imagines he resides in a realm beyond death, "thinking of new songs to play to her." Writing *Their Eyes Were Watching God* at a time in life when she was struggling with the issue of commitment to art and fidelity to romantic relationships, Hurston could not have made Janie a writer, for the novel would have seemed too much like autobiography. Even so, Janie is not an artist without an art form. She consciously approaches life as though it were a creative project, making no separation between life and art. In her life with Tea Cake, storytelling becomes the medium for the expression of her creativity. Like Tea Cake's music it is represented as a part of the dailiness of life.

Significantly, when Janie tells her story to Pheoby, it is as though she is painting a portrait. This story begins with uncertainty about representation. Janie cannot recognize her own image. Defined and named by others in childhood, Alphabet (as Janie is called then) cannot know or name herself. Ultimately her triumph in womanhood is that she acquires the ability to name and define her reality. Choosing to return to the house she owns, and the community she knows, after Tea Cake's death, Janie acknowledges that the muck was really his place. Bringing with her seeds to plant, a memento of her life with Tea Cake, a symbol of her love, she plants to nurture new life. Janie returns to her old community with new vision and insight. She is able to see the folks around her through the eyes of awareness. Self-realized, she need not experience interiority as confinement nor the outside world as threatening.

The courtroom scene was a crucial rite of passage for Janie. Just as she must privately prove that she has claimed her life by killing Tea Cake, she must be able to discursively defend her actions in public space. Publicly naming the radical subversive nature of her life and love with Tea Cake, Janie again risks her life. In the courtroom she is the ultimate outsider. Cut off by a blaming, unsupportive black community, she must confront a jury of "strange" white men. Janie stands alone. At the end of the trial Hurston incorporates a popular folk expression which claims that "Uh white man and uh nigger woman is de freest thing on earth" as an ironic gesture, highlighting all that Janie endures and suffers to be free. Of course the black men sharing this sentiment fail to understand her experience. Janie can survive the courtroom scene and Tea Cake's death because she has acquired an ontological framework on which to base the construction of self and identity. She can both speak the truth and live the truth of her experience. Sharing with Pheoby the importance of experience she bears witness:

> 'Course talkin' don't amount tuh uh hill uh beans when yuh can't do nothing else. And listenin' tuh dat kind uh talk is jus' lak openin' yo mouth and lettin' de moon shine down yo' throat. It's uh known fact, Pheoby, yo' got tuh go there. Yo' papa and yo' mama and nobody else can't tell yuh and show yuh. Two things everybody's tuh do fuh theyselves. They got tuh go tuh God, and they got tuh find out about livin' fuh theyselves.

Heterosexual bonding with Tea Cake enables Janie to fulfill her longing for romantic love and her quest for self-realization. Without embarrassment, Hurston suggests that poor black women victimized by gender discrimination must learn from men. She then suggests that having acquired necessary knowledge and skill, women can not only survive without men; we can flourish. The ending of *Their Eyes Were Watching God* would be problematic if Janie had returned home depressed and isolated. Though weary from her journey, she returns and reunites with her friend Pheoby. Mutually nourishing each other, Pheoby gives Janie food for the body and she gives her sustenance for the soul. When Pheoby tells Janie, "Ah done growed ten feet higher jus listenin' tuh you," the primacy of female bonding based on sharing knowledge is affirmed. Janie's quest for experience and knowledge does not lead her to abandon Pheoby. Hence just as Hurston rewrites the script of heterosexual romantic love, she insists that women need not be rivals as sexist norms suggest; instead, they can share power, reinforcing one another's autonomy. Janie shares her newfound "ideology of libera- tion" so that it can also have a transformative impact on Pheoby's life. Offered a new paradigm for heterosexual bonding, Pheoby can evaluate her life with Sam and suggest a new direction. Janie's power lies both in the ability to tell her story and the didactic impact of that telling.

Woolf ends *A Room of One's Own* by calling attention to the untapped creativity in all women and our capacity to nurture one another. Recognizing this to be an important stage in the process of self-development, but only a stage, she concludes by urging women to escape from isolation, from sex-segregated space. Her final charge is that women face "that there is no arm to cling to, but that we go alone and that our relation is to the world of reality, and not only to the world of men and women." Hurston ends the novel with a fictive mirroring of this prophetic declaration. It is an ending that celebrates woman's capacity to face life alone. Janie is not cut off from life. Possessing a keen memory and a powerful liberated imagination, she can create and be a world for herself. Last described in the act of reflection—Janie is thinking, remembering, imagining. Still rebellious, she challenges accepted perceptions of reality by positing a radically different way to view dying. Janie sees death not as an end to life but simply another stage of growth. Viewed from this perspective, death can be approached without fear, and the death of a loved one, though grievous, can become another ecstatic occasion where one bears witness to the unity of all life. It is this revelation that she witnesses at the end of the novel, that she calls "her soul to come and see."

As the novel ends, interiority is not depicted as a space of enclosure. It is not restrictive or confining. Janie opens windows, letting in air and light. Transformed interior space is expansive; it mirrors Janie's psyche. Importantly, the last paragraph reaffirms this transformation of inner domestic space. Janie has more than a room of her own, she has the capacity to live fully in that room—to resurrect, to reconcile, to renew. Janette Turner Hospital reminds us that Virginia Woolf's room of her own did not keep her alive. Hurston not only saves Janie's life, she gives her space to rest and renew her spirit, a space of infinite possibility, a space where she can create. Such a space, Hospital claims, is absolutely essential for the growth and development of the "female imagination":

> The quest for women writers then, and of their protagonists, is a search not just for a room of their own, but for safe private space, for non-toxic air, for a place where the self can really breathe. . . .

Hurston spent most of her life trying to find such a place. It was an unfulfilled quest. Without stones in her pocket, she, like Woolf, sank into the abyss, one the abyss of poverty and misfortune, the other madness and the suffocation of privilege that does not ensure freedom from pain. In *Their Eyes Were Watching God* Hurston creates this safe place—a wide transformative space Janie calls "home."

emily dickinson

the power of influence

When I imagine angels they are not some winged fantastical apparitions hanging on the rafters of the soul looking down. They are for me always embodied concrete guardians, those that the Ethiopian Coptics called *zars*. In the images the Coptics painted to give face to their beliefs angels are human-like. Angels were only useful in my childhood because they were guardians—there to see to the fulfillment of one's need, there to protect. I always chose my angels; sometimes they were real human beings and sometimes not. The angel of my solitary spirit, the one who guided me through poetry to the contemplative, to the mystical understanding that one could know the Divine through direct experience and encounter—this angel was Emily Dickinson.

Emily D., as I called her when I was ten years old, was certain of one thing, that solitude was essential for the nurturing of her creative imagination. Solitude was the space where her soul could come out of hiding and be heard. To talk with the world face to face, in the ordinary business of going out of one's house to shop, to meet—all of these disturbances would have sent the soul marooned to some place of forgetfulness. It would have been harder to find its intimacy again.

There was for Emily D. no better place to care for the soul than inside the home—the house of one's actual concrete daily living. Writing to her brother Austin in 1851 she shared: "Home is a holy thing—nothing of doubt or distrust can enter its blessed portals . . . here seems indeed to be a bit of Eden which not the sin of any can utterly destroy." In the Eden that was her home Emily Dickinson could subvert and defy all the restraints the world might have placed on her imagination and her being had she chosen to venture out more, had she chosen to live the normal life of a white woman of her times. Although I never thought of Emily D. in my childhood as white, I must do so now—to understand the luxury of her solitude, its privilege. No black woman of her day and time could have lived such a solitary life. In the world she lived in, black women were there to serve. These thoughts of race were never in my girlhood when Emily D., my sweet one, guardian and confidante, angel of my solitary spirit, spoke to me. Sharing the magic of stillness and contemplation, she spoke to me most clearly and directly in the shadowy spaces behind her words.

As a girl the only information about Emily D. we learned in school was that she rarely came out of the house. Her solitude was presented to us as weird, as a mark of her strangeness. It was the space behind the poems that offered the insight that there was more to this solitude, something deeper. To this poet who "dwelled in possibility" solitude was the place for magic and alchemy—the space wherein one could meet the Divine face to face.

When I read "This is my letter to the World / That never wrote to me—" I heard both lamentation and liberty. Emily D. seemed to both mourn her estrangement from the things of this world while exulting in the vision's seclusion and solitary confinement brought to her. That she mourns the very worldliness she has actively chosen to forego participation in to nurture her creative vision clearly shows concern and care for that world. To be at home in the world, Emily Dickinson needed to create a pure space where she could dream and dream without interruption, without needing to fear that the innocence of her vision would be corrupted. Without the distraction of worldliness, Dickinson could fully open the realm of her senses and sensually experience space both in the domestic household and in the natural world.

Living an ascetic, almost monastic existence she could hear more, see more of everything that was happening in nature. Dickinson's poems reveal her understanding of the interconnectedness of all living organisms. In Rosemary Reuther's ecofeminist theology of earth healing *Gaia and God* she asks: "How do we connect ourselves and the meaning of our lives to these worlds of the very small and the very big, standing in between the dancing void of energy that underlies the atomic structure of our bodies and the universe, whose galaxies, stretching over vast space and time, dwarf our histories. Even our bodies, despite the appearance of continuity over time, are continually dying and being reborn in every second." For Emily D. this connection was made by making a sacrament of the everyday, by remaining close to nature. Close enough to write of the inner life of flowers: "my nosegays are for captives; dim, long—expectant eyes, fingers denied the plucking, patient till paradise. to such, if they should whisper of morning and the moor, they bear no other errand. . . ." Or in "Forbidden Fruit": " 'Heaven'—is what I cannot reach! / The Apple on the tree—." Or when meditating on the meaning of storms in nature she writes "The Soul's Storm": "It struck me—every Day— / The Lightning was as new / As if the Cloud that instant slit / And let the Fire through—." In many poems Dickinson contemplates the ordinary visible things in our daily experiences—a bird, a flower, the next door neighbor's house, all of which become ways to arrive at a deeper transcendental meaning of the mystery and meaning of life.

Throughout my writing life, I have walked a creative path guided by the life and work of Emily Dickinson. Now as a mature woman and writer in retrospect I can see the myriad ways her commitment to solitude and contemplation deeply threaten patriarchal norms. That is why her solitariness is usually still presented to the minds of young girls and boys as something strange and weird. Even though time has accorded her an unchallenged place in the canon of "great" and serious American literature, the meaning of her solitude still remains suspect and unclear to many who read and appreciate her work. It is rarely presented as essential to the workings of her creativity in the same way that another poet who enthralled me during my girlhood, Rainer Maria Rilke's commitment to uninterrupted time is extolled as a sign of his devotion to his art, his willingness to lay down the ground of his worldly being to make that open space within wherein the poems could enter and the visionary voice speak. Dickinson's solitariness was essential for the cultivation of her creative passion. It was in that solitary space that she found her most intimate connection to the Divine, to that quality of yearning for ecstasy that would lead her to write "Wild Nights—Wild Nights!/ Were I with thee / Wild Nights should be / Our luxury!" Dickinson's poetry is a celebration of mystical union with the Divine. It is during those times that she is most "alone with the Alone" that her imagination takes flight and soars. It is that soaring in a world where there is no time and space that she, the angel of solitary spirits, finds us and stands watch over our creative spirit.

Working imaginatively to claim that space where we can

embrace contemplation and solitude, contemporary artists look to the presence of Emily Dickinson to inspire. Our engagement with her work connects us to one another. My journeying with Emily Dickinson brings me to the work of Roni Horn. In the fundamentalist Christian ethos of my childhood, supplicants would ask of the Divine to let "the breath of the Lord now breathe on me." This shared breath is symbolic of the passage of divine spirit from one being to another. Like mouth-to-mouth resuscitation it calls us back to life. Emily Dickinson's work has this life-sustaining power.

Horn acts to give visual expression to that power. By creating objects that embody the metaphysics inherent in Dickinson's vision and in her words, she both extends that breath and expands it. She opens up Dickinson, creating with, through, and beyond her. In her deconstructive appropriation of Dickinson, Horn maps out a visual typography of the contemplative imagination at work. To Horn, "mapping is a way of ordering things visually." In her typographic drawings and photographs there is a visual palimpsest that leads the eye back to the words underneath, the words and life of Dickinson that ground Horn's imaginative quest for a spatial frontier where solitude can reinvent itself within the postmodern context. Horn concentrates on Emily Dickinson's solitude, recognizing that this is the source of her genius and power. In the narrative "When Dickinson Shut Her Eyes," Horn reminds us that the poet lived "sequestered from the world" because she knew "that going out into the world hampered her ability to invent it." While she appropriates Dickinson's metaphysics of contemplation and solitude, Horn offers a vision of journeying that invites us to realize the possibility of a solitude we invent in spite of lives lived in a constantly frenetic and busy world. To return us to the quality of stillness lyrically evoked in Dickinson's poetics, Horn gives us the evocative object, sculptures of solid aluminum and plastic that urge a re-encountering of that contemplative stance. The sculpture "Key and Cue, No. 351" stands straight; against a plain, sparse backdrop a single declarative statement asserts: "I FELT MY LIFE WITH BOTH MY HANDS." Or the "Untitled" piece—cubes stacked that compel us to look and hear again Dickinson's words: "MY LIFE HAS STOOD A LOADED GUN." These sculptures have a purity of presence that insists on a world where all that is unnecessary has been stripped away.

In her life and work Emily Dickinson stripped away the excess, the clutter, to make room for clarity. The meditative quality of her words resonates in the images Horn creates to contain and further illuminate that world. The closeness Horn feels with Emily Dickinson, one that defies time and space, impressed itself on her imagination. Reading Dickinson's letters and poems she found in the work a place of recognition, a mirroring of her own inner landscape. A geography of the heart began to imprint itself on Horn's imagination. She would enter more fully into the psychic spaces inhabited by Emily Dickinson to return to herself, and her present. Horn's work is not sentimental or nostalgic. It is a careful analytical imaginative mapping of an inner geography of soul—and the reaching through time of one artist toward another. Articulating this sense of space in the text "Anatomy and Geography" included in *Pooling Waters*, Horn shares the insight that "inner geography is a plain knowledge of oneself, a kind of common sense gathered through repeated exposure to distilling experiences. Inner geography maps peace of mind in the world as it is and not as I imagine it." Like Dickinson, Horn's approach is that of the documentary observer, the surveyor who through a systematic process of looking allows the landscape to reveal itself without the imposition of a predetermined view. She fixates on the landscape of Dickinson's imagination, doubling this with her concern for an inner geography that transcends that landscape, that makes it over so that it becomes a new site, a new place. Both "When Dickinson Shut Her Eyes" and "How Dickinson Stayed Home" remind us that located at the site of this inner geography are multiple narratives, diverse points of entry. Unlike Dickinson, who was always mapping an inner geography with the spatial constraints of confinement and containment, Horn moves beyond the realm of domestic space, across the globe, to observe, to chart those traces of an inner geography hidden behind the outer busy world of action, change, and ongoing movement. Horn, in her own words, stresses that she "uses the outer world to notate the inner." Artistically, she offers a revisionist perspective on both Dickinson and her work that interrogates the intensity of her solitariness even as it visually attests to the power of stillness, of contemplation.

Roni Horn's work demands of audiences direct engagement. We must look both backwards to see the impact of Dickinson and forward into the unique artistic representation of that impact. Horn's work calls attention to the primacy of solitude even as it reminds us that the outcome of engaged solitude is an intensification of a sense of togetherness. In the writings of religious mystics globally there is a constant emphasis on the way in which solitude enables solidarity. Theologian William McNamara clarifies this understanding: "Discreet solitude is a creative protest against the euphoric or chaotic togetherness that stamps our way of life in the modern world. But it is also the highest and most apt expression of our solidarity with the whole human race, with the whole of creation. The more solitary we are, the more divinely endowed and psychologically equipped to enter a significantly profound relationship with all levels of life— animal, vegetable, mineral as well as human." Horn seeks to capture that point of entry, to explore the unseen aspects of the contradictions between our desire for connectedness and our longing for spaces that are solitary. Acknowledging both her connection to Dickinson and the way that bond enables a movement out—across boundaries in "When Dickinson Shut Her Eyes"—she creates a journal-like narrative recording: "For the time being, Dickinson's here with me, in Iceland. For someone who stayed home she fits naturally into this distant and necessary place. Her writing is an equivalent of this unique island; Dickinson invented a syntax out of herself, and Iceland did too. Volcanos do. Dickinson stayed home to get at the world. But home is an island like this one. And I come to this island to get at the very center of the world." From this location, at the center, Horn is able to look into the heart of the matter and envision a visual montage of landscapes that allows all of us to come closer to Iceland, to that inner Island, without ever having to leave the spaces we call home. This act of remembering, of connecting that which appears to be disparate, separate echoes the thoughts expressed in the last stanza of Dickinson's poem "The Forgotten Grave": "Winds of summer fields / Recollect the Way,— / Instinct picking up the key / Dropped by Memory." Horn's work gives us a key—a way to open up the doors of our memory so that a space exists where we travel in and through time.

Her work evokes the poetic lyricism of a past that merges with the present so effortlessly that there is no separation in time. Every moment is a present moment. And it is there in that complete and utter surrender to the present that life is found. It is their devotion to the present moment that is the metaphysical link between Dickinson and Horn. Within Buddhist teachings, works like the Avatamsaka Sutra remind us that returning to the present is the only way to be in contact with life. Interpreting the sutra, Thich Nhat Hanh shares that "time and space are not separate," that "time is made up of space, and space is made up of time." Horn's sculptures urge the onlooker to engage fully with the present. To read the scripts—the messages passed through time—we must be fully aware, mindful in that moment when we confront the art itself. They draw us into the tranquillity of stillness as we observe deeply the image. The joining of physical objects with narrative is a conceptual strategy that calls our attention to dialogical acts of communion that are sacramental.

Indeed, as we look as this work, we bear witness to the communion of souls that takes place between Dickinson and Horn. The reality that this communion remains vibrant and interactive even though these two artists never met in the flesh challenges the conventional notion that death ends communication. The Harlem Boys Choir sings a song with the lyrics "There is no death for an angel." There is definitely an insistence on the primacy of the immortal in Horn's work, substances that will not lose their properties through time but merely undergo various conversions. That hint of immortality, both in the emotional bond she feels with Dickinson and in the work, the traces of love that linger, bind her both to worlds she has never known and those brave new worlds she journeys to. That palimpsest is a mapping of an inner geography that is such a powerful force, it can bring together three women from diverse backgrounds with different histories, who walk different paths, and connect us—Dickinson, Horn, hooks. In our shared immersion in the sacrament of solitude we are renewed, our spirits uplifted. Henri Nouwen writes in his meditation *Out of Solitude* that the experience of solitude enables us to "slowly unmask the illusion of our possessiveness and discover in the center of our own self that we are not what we can conquer, but what is given to us." Horn's work exults in the sharing of these gifts.

the legacy of ann petry

Long before feminist theorists began to think in terms of race, gender, and class, black women writers had created work that spoke from this previously unarticulated standpoint. Describing in their fictions the ways sex, race, and class work as interlocking systems of domination, Harriet Jacobs, Zora Neale Hurston, and Nella Larsen were among those exceptional visionaries providing ways to understand black female experience that could not be found in print anywhere else. Among this work, Ann Petry's novel *The Street* was groundbreaking. Read by millions, it showed the world the ways forces of sexism (including patriarchal domination of men over men), racism, and class oppression specifically shaped the nature of black female experience. Confrontational, *The Street* is hard-hitting. It has the power to knock readers off their feet. I see it happen again and again when I teach the novel in classes on black women writers. I see students awakening to the realization of the way systems of domination can work to exploit and oppress. I see them developing insights about the nature of poor black female experience that they previously did not have and feeling an empathic concern for social change that mirrors Lutie's longings in the novel.

The republication of *The Street* in paperback by its original publisher, Houghton Mifflin, has helped to create a contemporary public context where the work can receive renewed attention and the author Ann Petry can be celebrated once again. Amid all the stories we must tell again and again of black women writers whose lives were full of tragedy, abuse, brokenheartedness, unrelenting physical or psychological pain, or unceasing loneliness, it is crucial that we tell with as much passion and soulfulness the triumphant stories of the Ann Petrys of this world—that we celebrate black women writers who live long and well, whose histories are life affirming and life sustaining. Indeed, we are so accustomed to tragic autobiographical narratives of black female life that it is easy to overlook an Ann Petry. Yet she is the living embodiment of Hurston's declaration "But I am not tragically colored. There is no great sorrow dammed up in my soul, nor lurking behind my eyes. . . . No, I do not weep at the world—I am too busy sharpening my oyster knife." Elegant at eighty-three years old, Petry lived with her husband George in the quaint New England town of Old Saybrook. Her house is one of those tender wood-framed dwellings that you drive by on a sunny afternoon and long to know who lives there. You are convinced by the serenity surrounding this dwelling that it is a house that breeds contentment, that offers comfort. When I shyly entered Ann Petry's house a few years ago, I felt like I was coming home. There was a warmth in that two-hundred-year-old dwelling so familiar to me that it was as if I were simply returning to visit one of those dear black women teachers in my hometown who gave us so much wisdom, who educated for critical consciousness, who loved us.

But as the old folks say, I'm getting ahead of myself. I want to backtrack for a minute and remember how it was that I came to meet Miss Petry (even though I knew she was married I could not address her as Ann and she just seemed to be the type of black woman elder whom you always want to address with the appropriate amount of respect as Miss Petry). My first full-time teaching job was in Connecticut at Yale University. Hundreds of students flocked to my course on black women writers. I mentioned to my ever-knowledgable landlady Ruth that I was teaching Ann Petry and she shared with me that the writer lived nearby in Old Saybrook. My stunned reply was, "You mean to say she's still alive!" I climbed the steep flights of stairs to my apartment and found to my amazement that a telephone operator gave me her home number. Daring to do what I had never done before, I called her. There was such awe and amazement in my voice when she answered and confirmed that she was indeed living that I was stumbling over my words. In my polite southern Sunday-school voice (one that is often hidden but surfaces whenever I am in a context that triggers that sense of the familiarity of home), I shared my love of her work, the joy of teaching it, and the desire to have my students be in her presence. Thrilled when she agreed to come talk to our class, I conveyed to my students that we were among the "chosen" to have an opportunity to hear Ann Petry's voice, to be in her presence. It was crucial for me as a contemporary black woman writer to challenge the notion that "we" all die miserable, young, and poor.

Later, over tea and wonderful bread (made by her husband, George) she shared that it was the sound of my voice that seduced her into making a rare public appearance. This brought to my mind memories of my first "grand passion," the love letter he wrote that declared it was the sense of song in my voice that enthralled. Visiting Ann Petry and meeting her husband one encountered a real-life love story that challenges all those homegrown stereotypes that suggest a talented, powerful black woman will always have trouble finding a mate. Listening to them tell the story of how they met, of moving to New York in 1938 so George could manage a restaurant and Ann could pursue her passion for writing, sparks of their initial romantic bonding showed the love that lingered. Petry attributed finding heterosexual happiness to learning from generations of women in her family that it is best for a woman to choose only a partner who really adores and admires you. Her mother and aunts all married men who adored them. Petry commented: "I imagine if my mother or her sisters said, 'Lie down and let me walk on you,' these men probably would have—and said it felt good." Petry was not suggesting that domination of one person over the other represents the ideal, or that black women are better off if we dominate and control black men. She was suggesting that when a man adores a woman within the framework of patriarchy he is already moving against the conventional sexist grain that suggests men should fear women and therefore control us. Such a man is more willing to engage in a mutual relationship, one that is constructed so that both partners can be fulfilled. George Petry has that personal confidence that makes sharing space with a powerful black woman possible. And both shared a good sense of humor. Together they made their home a place of laughter and delight.

It is not surprising that folks who had the good fortune to encounter Ann Petry there wondered how such a serene presence could have imagined the harsh violent world depicted in *The Street*. Coming from a loving black family, one that knew material comfort despite racism, Petry was especially positioned to be horrifed by the way racism and poverty together created a politics of everyday life that was and is genocidal to black folks. It was as witness to this genocide as a young writer in Harlem observing the world around her that she was compelled to write a novel that would not only describe the conditions there but also be a statement of protest, one that would urge readers to change their attitudes. Petry, more than most black writers, highlights issues of class in her work. Teaching *The Street* I have wanted students to consider the way in which her standpoint as a privileged sheltered New England black girl informed the way she fictively imagined life to be on those Harlem streets. Yet students were so awed by her presence in the classroom that they were unable to address with her issues of class.

When she entered the classroom, the space was packed with my students and all these other folks who had come to honor Ann Petry. Dwarfed by so many bodies Ann Petry suddenly appreared fragile. I was afraid that this event might be too taxing. Yet, when she began to speak the passion in her voice rocked the room. Without batting an eye, she revealed that she knew before putting pen to paper that Lutie would murder Boots. Hearing this hurt. Many of us felt the deep truth of her words. We knew from our own life experiences that often when black folks are wounded and downpressed by racism, class oppression, sexist exploitation our rage explodes in relation to other black folks.

The Street is a portrait of black rage. Long before psychiatrists Grier and Cobbs, in *Black Rage*, wrote about the fierce anger that so many black people keep bottled up within, Ann Petry's character told readers: "Every day we are choking down that rage." In many ways Lutie is constructed as a typically feminine woman of the forties, who dreams of having a nice house, a storybook family. It is only as a worker in the white world that she begins to "awaken" to the way poor attractive black females without money are seen by white folks: "Apparently it was an automatic reaction of white people—if a girl was colored and fairly young, why, it stood to reason she had to be a prostitute. If not that—at least sleeping with her would be just a simple matter, for all one had to do was make the request. In fact, white men wouldn't even have to do the asking because the girl would ask them on sight." This 1940s novel had such an impact on its audience because Lutie could be any struggling poor American trying to realize the dream of working hard and struggling to achieve economic success. She does not want to be rich. In fact, the novel exposes the emptiness and unhappiness in the lives of the rich. No, Lutie just wants a good job and a nice place to live. And she is willing to work hard. Yet, Petry skillfully shows that the politics of domination work to undermine and ultimately destroy Lutie's ambition.

In keeping with the progressive political fiction of her day, Petry wants readers to understand that there is no inherent defect in Lutie or other poor black people. That the very "real" forces of poverty and capitalist exploitation exploit and oppress. The black and white people who survive and "make it" in *The Street* are those who are willing to accept the idea that it is a dog-eat-dog world, those who prey upon others. Mrs. Hedges, who becomes a madam, or Junto, the rich white man who finances the "pleasures" of the street, reveal that it is those who throw aside dreams of fulfillment and adapt to harsh realities who make it. Petry's novel was a veiled critique of capitalism, crass materialism, and the dehumanization of American citizens. When Lutie goes to Children's Court to see her son Bub who has been arrested for tampering with the mail, she finds that it is not just "colored" women who suffer from a society that supports the rich and crushes the poor: "She had been wrong. There were some white mothers, too. . . . They were sitting in the same shrinking, huddled positions. Perhaps, she thought, we're all here because we're all poor. Maybe it doesn't have anything to do with color." Through her experience Lutie learns about sexism (that the young black musician Boots and the rich white man Junto both believe that they should have access to her body with or without her consent, that they are both willing to use coercion). She learns daily about racism (again and again she expresses her awareness that white supremacy and hatred of blackness create a system where black folks are victimized). And she learns about class exploitation. Ultimately, Lutie must lose the "innocence" that has shielded her from the harsh realities of the street. Petry's portrait of Lutie's naïveté is somewhat unbelievable. Her fictional unawareness seems to belong more to the middle-class observer of poor black life in Harlem than to Lutie. As Liz, Ann Petry's daughter, puts it: "*The Street* upset me dreadfully when I was young. My mother really is a very upbeat person, and I was surprised that it was so down. I can only guess at what she went through when she moved to New York and saw all these disenfranchised people, totally lacking power in a way that she and our family never did." Even though Petry uses the character of Lutie to express some of her middle-class "horror" at the harsh reality of poor black life, it does not diminish the power of *The Street*. And she does not create a fiction where readers (and white readers specifically) are encouraged to identify with Lutie as the character who has aspiring middle-class values while condemning other characters.

The Street is powerful precisely because Petry does not suggest that all poor people will respond in the same way when faced with social circumstances that would dehumanize. Mrs. Hedges is one of the heroic characters in *The Street*. Readers are encouraged to admire her not because she embodies conventional morality. She lives by the rules of street cultures. We are encouraged to admire her because she is able to use the resources in the environment around her to survive. Unlike Lutie, Mrs. Hedges does not feel trapped in the street. She feels at home there. Accepting the philosophy that "only the strong survive," Mrs. Hedges adapts to the environment and triumphs over adversity. As readers we can applaud her triumph and yet also lament the narrowness of her vision. She has no place to dream of going, no world of family and kin to return to. Only in this way is she a tragic figure. Like the Super, who is portrayed as the most completely dehumanized by his environment, Mrs. Hedges is afraid of a world beyond the street. Even though she has enough money to leave the street and live elsewhere she chooses to stay. Like Min, the Super's live-in partner, these black women know how to adapt to harsh circumstances and yet change those circumstances. As a result they are not isolated and estranged like Lutie. And it is Lutie's isolation that makes her more vulnerable to sexist exploitation.

With her characterization of Boots Smith, and Lutie's husband Jim, Petry creates a graphic portrait of the way sexism converges with racism and class exploitation, perverting and distorting black gender relations. Treated as objects by the larger society all the black characters risk internalizing this thinking and treating one another as objects. This is most evident in Boots's relationship to Lutie. When Junto, the rich white male "boss," lets him know that he wants Lutie, Boots must decide whether he will act in complicity or attempt to rescue Lutie. It is that moment in the novel when he examines the impact of racism on his social circumstance, weighing a return to a form of poverty that makes him as a black man more likely to suffer abuse at the hands of white people over the desire to protect Lutie, which most graphically shows the way class oppression, racism, and sexism together undermine the possibility that humanizing redemptive love will win out over a politics of domination. Boots thinks: "Balance Lutie Johnson. Weigh Lutie Johnson. . . . Not enough. She didn't weigh enough when she was balanced against a life of saying 'yes sir' to every white bastard who had the price of a Pullman ticket."

Concurrently, in order for Lutie to murder Boots she must see him solely as an object. When she strikes out it is not at Boots

Smith "but at a handy, anonymous figure—a figure which her angry resentment transformed into everything she had hated, everything she had fought against, everything that had served to frustrate her." Both of them ultimately objectify and dehumanize the other. What made Petry's novel so shocking was that she gave the center stage not to the angry black male but to a type of black female that most people do not see as harboring rage. Yet, Lutie is consumed by anger and rage. Despite the novel's sad ending, it is the expression of that rage that awakens Lutie, destroying the fantasies and dreams that have rendered her unable to respond in a productive way to the reality of her life. We do not know how Lutie will live when the novel ends. We do know that she no longer believes in the idealized myth of the American Dream. And that no clinging to this myth will enable her to face reality in a way that will allow her to grow and mature.

The tragedy of exploitation and oppression Ann Petry described in 1946 is more than ever a common experience for black people and black women in particular. White people in this country continue to deny the traumatic impact of white supremacy. And only recently have we been able to examine the way race, sex, and class together determine individual social circumstance. Interviewed by Marc Fisher for the *Washington Post* Petry acknowledged that she saw little change in race relations: "The relationship between blacks and whites in this country is worse now than it's ever been." Hopefully, contemporary readers of *The Street* will leave the work with greater awareness of the nature of sex, race, and class oppression. And that this awareness will lead them to work to transform society and the street, so that the warmth and contentment Ann Petry was able to offer her loved ones and those strangers (like myself) who had the good fortune to enter her world will be there for everyone.

Meeting with Ann Petry, I began to think critically about the way mass media constructs the image of "the black woman writer." Not only was it heartwarming to encounter a famous black female writer who did not feel a need to trash younger writers to emphasize her specialness, it was inspirational to be in the presence of a black female who was never swept away by the forces of stardom. All along the way, Ann Petry made choices that reflected a primary concern with her well-being and that of her loved ones. That was a courageous stance at a time when many folks were pressuring her to become a spokesperson, to be in the limelight. Without giving up her commitment to writing, Petry chose to leave the limelight and live life on her own terms. This is a special gift. Few black women have offered such a powerful legacy to younger black female writers trying to chart contemporary journeys for ourselves and our work. Her death, after a long and fulfilling life, is a tremendous loss to those of us who cherished her presence as well as her written words. Those words are the legacy given us to keep and hold dear—now and always.

hansberry

the deep one

Even though I knew as a girl that I wanted to be a writer, it took years for me to discover a black woman writer whose life and work inspired me and affirmed my aspirations. Even though I discovered black women writers in my teens, I knew nothing of their lives and work habits. I entered college with a drama scholarship, seeing myself as destined to be both actress and writer. During my first year of study I went to see a performance of Lorraine Hansberry's *To Be Young, Gifted and Black*. I was already familiar with her play *A Raisin in the Sun* from my high school drama classes. Although I enjoyed this earlier play, seeing myself mirrored in the character of Beneatha, it seemed then like very conventional drama. I did not come away from the play wondering about the life of the playwright—who she was, where she was coming from, why she chose to write plays.

Having recently left the world of the segregated South to come all the way to Stanford University and study drama, I felt utterly alienated from the world around me. Everything was new and strange. When I saw *To Be Young, Gifted and Black*, a play bearing witness to the reality of Hansberry's life and work, I felt that I was no longer alone. She had experienced intense alienation when she went away to college. She did not fit. Her struggles with sexuality and love were problematic. Hansberry was fascinated by global politics, women's liberation, black power. She was "in the mix." After seeing the performance I began to read everything I could find about her life and work. Awed by the intimate portrayal of Hansberry "the artist" in *To Be Young, Gifted and Black*, I returned to my dormitory room that night ecstatic because I had found a new literary mentor.

At the time, Hansberry's dying young made her seem all the more romantic. She represented the "new woman"—the woman I wanted to become. Experimental, free, determined to live life on her own terms. I wept over scenes from her play *The Sign in Sidney Brustein's Window*. Her dramatic portrait *Toussaint* taught me to consider the fate of black resistance historically in relation to our individual and collective will to sacrifice for freedom. *Les Blancs* led me to think about Africa, imperialism, and colonialism. Hansberry was the only young black woman artist I had found who was a critical thinker interested in feminism and in the global politics of race and nation. In an article written in 1963, "On Arthur Miller, Marilyn Monroe, and 'Guilt,' " Hansberry reveals the scope of her political thinking and her metaphysical beliefs. Her comments are worth quoting at length:

> Things are very, very complicated. . . . But they aren't *that* complicated either. The English [colonialists] are wrong, the Kikuyu [rebelling subjects] are right; we are wrong. Castro is right; the Vietnamese people (there doesn't appear to be any difference between the Vietnamese people and the 'Viet

Cong' any more by our own account) are right and we are wrong; the Negro people are right and the shameful dawdling of Federal authority [in securing their civil rights] is wrong, the concept of 'woman' which fashioned, warped and destroyed a human being such as Marilyn Monroe (or 'Audrey Smith' or 'Jean West' or 'Lucy Jones'—daily) IS HIDEOUSLY WRONG—and she, *in her repudiation of it*, in trying tragically to RISE ABOVE it by killing herself is (in the Shakespearean sense)—right.

A woman of courage and daring, Hansberry had no trouble taking a stand for what she believed was right action.

Hansberry's work entered my life just as I was grappling with the difficult question of whether or not I could be both writer and intellectual; when I was trying to figure out if I could be a part of feminist movement and still play a part in the struggle for black liberation. Through her work, she became a guiding light. A woman of paradox, from Hansberry I learned to accept multiple locations as points of identification. She loved and celebrated the specific culture of black America, embracing the African diaspora even as she also loved the best writing from European authors. Who could not be enchanted by a writer responding to a letter from a white midwestern farm boy by writing: "I suppose I think that the highest gift that man has is art, and I am audacious enough to think of myself as an artist, that there is both joy and beauty and illumination and communion between people to be achieved through the dissection of personality. That's what I want to do. I want to reach a little closer to the world, which is to say people, and see if we can share some illuminations together about each other." I identified more with Hansberry than with other black women writers because she had both a distinct commitment to an artistic vision realized with literary excellence as well as an ongoing commitment to social and political activism. Hansberry remains a radical visionary, an artist whose intellectual work has not received the attention and level of recognition that would have been hers long ago had she been born a man.

When I enter classrooms to teach American literature, especially writing by black women, I want students to leave knowing the work of Lorraine Hansberry. Many students have never heard her name. Among those who have, few have seen a staged production of any of her plays, or the film versions of *A Raisin in the Sun*. Even though *American Playhouse* presented this play to millions of television viewers, audiences are prone to quickly forget the contributions of black women writers. Those of us who will never forget were thrilled that she received this tribute to her work. She remains for us a guiding force. While she was a gifted playwright, that was not the sole measure of her brilliance. She was both artist and intellectual, a critical thinker concerned with the pressing social issues of her time. Her essays and creative writing reveal to contemporary readers that she was a radical visionary, her work prophetic.

Unlike many contemporary writers, including black authors, Hansberry never ignored political issues. Her compelling and forceful 1959 essay "The Negro Writer and His Roots: Towards a New Romanticism" was delivered at a conference about black writers convened by the American Society of African Culture. At this conference she urged black artists and intellectuals to recognize the vital connection between politics and aesthetics. Calling for direct engagement, Hansberry dared black writers to seize power and address a wide range of cultural and political concerns: "The foremost enemy of the Negro intelligentsia of the past has been and in a large sense remains—isolation. No more than can the Negro people afford to imagine themselves removed from the most pressing world issues of our time—war and peace, colonialism, capitalism vs. socialism—than can I believe that the Negro writer imagines that he will be exempt from artistic examination of questions which plague the intellect and spirit of man." This essay remains one of the most significant discussions of the relationship between art and politics. In this piece Hansberry reminds everyone "that all art is ultimately social."

For many years *A Raisin in the Sun* was my least favorite of Hansberry's plays because it seemed on the surface to be conservative. Yet the *American Playhouse* production included parts of the play that had been taken out years ago. The parts that were removed were those that graphically portrayed radical politics. Retrospectively, audiences can accept Hansberry's concern with the global politics of U.S. imperialism, colonialism, and the question of African independence. Today, her interest in feminist questions seems utterly normal. Yet these were the issues that had to be toned down for a fifties audience. Ironically, then, many audiences saw the play as affirming the notion that black women are matriarchal heads of black households. Yet Hansberry's play was celebrating just the opposite. There is ongoing insistence in the play that Lena Younger assumes her position as head of the household only because her husband Big Walter is dead. Constant dramatic evocation of his presence emphasizes that the values and beliefs they shared as a couple inform the decision she makes after his death.

Most critics failed to call attention to this subplot—the love story of Big Walter and Lena. Yet the fictional portrait of Big Walter directly challenges racist and sexist assumptions about black masculinity, about the role of black men as workers. Significantly, Lena constantly praises Big Walter's work ethic, even suggesting that he died young because he worked too hard. In the television production Esther Rolle's interpretation of Lena's character is truly magnificent. No longer portrayed stereotypically as a fierce black matriarch, she is reserved and resolute. Yet we also see her vulnerability, the way the various crises she confronts affect her emotionally. We see how she critically reflects on her actions and changes them. It is a powerful dramatic moment when she confesses to Walter Lee (her son) her complicity in denying him the opportunity to act as a responsible adult person. An engaging aspect of this production is the extent to which individual characters are portrayed in a completely multidimensional manner, not as flat stereotypes.

Certainly the character of Beneatha (played by Kim Yancey) was a radical portrayal of an emerging feminist. This production was the first one that did not downplay her role, subordinating it to Mrs. Younger and Walter Lee. One of the most moving moments in the play occurs when Beneatha explains to her sister-in-law Ruth and her mother the need for women to express themselves. Their sweet contemptuous laughter highlights the gulf separating these generations of black women. Beneatha's struggle to find an adequate language to articulate her emergent revolutionary black female identity prophetically shows the struggle to be self-defining facing black youth today. Much contemporary feminist scholarship explores the relationship between mothers and daughters both in fiction and everyday life. The characterization of the mother/daughter bond in *A Raisin in the Sun* is an unusual fictive portrayal of affirmation between black women. In much of the work by black women writers mothers fail to prepare their daughters to live a different and/or better life. They neglect and abandon them, never giving sustained emotional care.

Even though Lena Younger is old-fashioned, by no means a "new woman," she wholeheartedly nurtures and supports Beneatha in all her endeavors—the silly and the serious. Their relationship is deeply loving and full of contradictions. Beneatha respects her mother's power yet feels she is tyrannical sometimes. A dramatic confrontation between mother and daughter occurs when Beneatha expresses her anger and rejection of her brother Walter Lee. This is the moment in the play when Lena Younger offers her metaphysical understanding of the meaning of compassion: "You—you mourning your brother? You feeling like you better than he is today? What you tell him a minute ago? That he wasn't a man? Yes? You give him up for me? You done wrote his epitaph too—like the rest of the world? Well, who give you the privilege? Child, when do you think is the time to love somebody the most: when they done good and made things easy for everybody? Well then, you ain't through learning—because that ain't the time at all. It's when he's at his lowest and can't believe in hisself 'cause the world done whipped him so. When you starts measuring somebody, measure him right, child, measure him right. Make sure you done taken into account what hills and valleys he come through before he got to wherever he is. . . ." Passages like this one reveal Hansberry's gift with language and her desire to portray the profundity and wisdom that Lena has gleaned from her experience, which is symbolic of collective black experience. Her plays allowed audiences to hear the poetic lyrical nuances of black vernacular.

Hansberry wanted audiences to reconsider the standards used to judge and dismiss working-class folks, particularly the black working class. In a radio interview with Studs Terkel she identified her middle-class roots while expressing solidarity with the black masses: "I guess at this moment the Negro middle class—the comfortable middle class—may be from five to six percent of our people, and they are atypical of the representative experience of Negroes in this country. Therefore, I have to believe that whatever we ultimately achieve, however we ultimately transform our lives, the changes will come from the kind of people I chose to portray. They are more pertinent, move relevant, more significant—most important, more decisive—in our political history and our political future." She was equally fascinated by the lives of white people across class. Her black identity did not mean that she could not make white characters center stage. Despite her focus on whiteness, she was most fascinated by the way in which black people, her people, had survived racist exploitation and oppression.

Hansberry was impressed by the dignity and beauty of black life, urging young black writers to "write about our people: tell their story." *A Raisin in the Sun* is a uniquely American drama. It paved the way for future black playwrights, like August Wilson, providing them a platform to demand that theater audiences recognize the heroic elements of black experience. The issues raised in *A Raisin in the Sun* are as relevant today as they were when the play was first performed. Its contemporary relevance is indicative of the prophetic nature of Hansberry's experience. In his introduction to *To Be Young, Gifted and Black* James Baldwin recalled the moment when black viewers came backstage to see Lorraine Hansberry after the initial production of her first successful play. He declared her to be more than an artist; she was a "witness." He also shared that to bear witness was difficult and risky. Despite the critical acclaim Hansberry received for her work, she was also criticized. According to Baldwin's account, white and black folks criticized her "very harshly, very loudly." While they were never able to silence her words, they did cause her great distress. At times she felt extremely isolated and alone even though she continued to write and be politically active.

As a dissident voice, Lorraine Hansberry stands alone. Few black women writers have been as radical as she was. In keeping with her daring manner she wrote a letter to the *New York Times* defending black radicalism, which they refused to publish. She addressed a forum on "The Black Revolution and the White Backlash." Speaking with fellow writers about the issues of solidarity between whites and blacks she stated: "The problem is we have to find some way, with these dialogues, to encourage the white liberal to stop being a liberal—and become an American radical." Hansberry insisted: "I don't think we can decide ultimately on the basis of color. The passion that we express should be understood, I think, in that context. We want total identification. It's not a question of reading anybody out; it's a merger . . . but it has to be on the basis of true and genuine equality. And if we think that isn't going to be painful, we're mistaken. . . ." One of the first black writers to publish in openly gay magazines, Hansberry linked feminism and gay rights long before it was popular to do so. Yet in typical eclectic fashion she also critiqued the sexism of gay males. In an unpublished letter to a gay magazine she wrote: "The relationship of anti-homosexual sentiment to the oppression of women has a special and deep implication. That is to say that the reason for the double standard of social valuation is rooted in the societal contempt for the estate of womanhood in the first place."

Hansberry's activism gave necessary support to her artistic assertions about the future of humankind—her optimism. With visionary foresight she saw that black and white people alike would lose hope. She saw that nihilism and despair could destroy black liberation struggle in the diaspora. All her writing is deeply optimistic. Her work is hopeful, yet that hope is never based on false sentimentality. It is always rooted in activism. She saw change and knew it was possible to envision and make a better society. Hansberry transgressed boundaries at a time when it was not acceptable to cross borders. Looking at the world from a standpoint that recognized the interconnectedness of race, sex, and class, she challenged everyone who encountered her work. While Hansberry's vision is clear in *To Be Young, Gifted and Black*, hopefully there will come a day when her essays, interviews, and speeches will be published more widely and therefore become more well known.

A few weeks ago a talented, brilliant young black woman student came to see me and complained about isolation, about the absence of radical intellectual comrades. She wanted to know what I did during times of depression when I feel dispirited and alone. I told her I often turn to the work of Lorraine Hansberry to renew my spirit, to remind me that I am not alone. Hansberry died at the tender age of thirty-four. Before her death she wrote with intensity and devotion. She wrote about her passion for life. That passion remains visible in the work. It is restorative. Hansberry will always be a guiding light. As an intellectual and a writer I walk a path that she first cleared. Few writers give that much.

writing with grace

the magic of morrison

"When I think of autumn I think of hands that do not want me to die." This is what the impoverished little black girl Claudia thinks in *The Bluest Eye*, Toni Morrison's first novel, when she is sick with cold. Feeling all alone and uncared for until her mother appears and rubs soothing salve into her chest to make her better, Claudia knows these hands are full of healing power, full of longing for her to be made well. I love this sentence because it does so much with so little. Morrison's writing is like that. She is able to take the simplest combination of words and put them together in a way that astounds, that awes as readers confront a depth and complexity beyond anything they can express in language. The sheer lyrical beauty of her language seduces and enchants us, even if we do not feel in agreement with the vision of the world she fictively evokes. We come away from her writing with images and passages in our heads that we listen to over and over again, the way song lyrics linger in our memory through time, songs that are unforgettable.

To be a contemporary writer whose work has such power is

already to inhabit the space of the elect, the chosen. Overwhelming reader response reminds the world that this writing has sustained literary power. It is in keeping with that power that the world pays homage, that Toni Morrison's work can receive a Nobel Prize. Her work has always been special—set apart. Publishing her first book much later in her career than young writers today, Morrison entered the literary scene at a time when contemporary feminist movement was calling attention to works by women writers and suddenly paying attention to writing by black women. As literary women worked to uncover the buried histories of writing about women they noticed first the way black women writers were almost ignored, their presence all but erased from the literary cultural landscape.

Significantly, black women writers of the twenties and thirties, Zora Neale Hurston, Nella Larsen, Ann Petry, whose books attracted a large reading public when first published, had long been forgotten by mainstream audiences. Feminist presses took the lead in uncovering and reclaiming this material. Almost singlehandedly Alice Walker used her literary power in feminist circles to call attention to Hurston's work. Luckily, feminist efforts to recover women's history, lost life stories and fictions, helped shine a contemporary spotlight on the works of little-known black women writers of the past. The demand for women's words led to greater focus on contemporary writers who had already been publishing before feminist movement.

In the early seventies many young women readers first read Toni Morrison's work in classes taught by feminist professors. *The Bluest Eye*, followed by *Sula*, was on every reading list. Long before mainstream audiences collectively celebrated the work of Toni Morrison, before her writing was extolled and canonized in academic settings, she was chosen by feminist readers. I was one of those readers. As an aspiring young writer from a working-class background looking for ways to articulate the life I most intimately knew, I found affirmation and inspiration in Toni Morrison's work. Her writing influenced me more than other women writers whose work emerged more directly from the feminist world because she was obsessed with craft. It was clear that she used language with a precision and skill that made a mockery of any attempt to dismiss this writing as merely a pale imitation of "great male writers."

In the late seventies mainstream culture was definitely changing its perceptions of women writers and their work. While traditional English departments began to include Toni Morrison's fiction on course syllabi, there was still a degree of ambivalence. Indeed, when I made the decision to write my dissertation on her first two novels, my advisors were not wholeheartedly supportive. At the time they expressed concern that she did not yet have the literary stature that would merit concentrated scholarly attention culminating in a book-length manuscript. Also they were worried that it would make me a less desirable candidate on the job market to focus on a contemporary writer, and more specifically a black woman writer. I was eager to take the risk because my engagement with Toni Morrison's work was so intense. It was not the unproblematic engagement of a fan, wanting to celebrate her favorite writer. I loved Morrison's writing style even as I believed that her work demanded the same critical evaluation and interrogation that we were giving Ernest Hemingway, William Faulkner, James Joyce, or a lesser-known writer like Kate Chopin. All useful critique must necessarily do more than celebrate.

I wish I could say that my choice to write on Toni Morrison's work was prophetic. It was not. I chose to write about her novels simply because I loved the work and believed it deserved a level of sophisticated critical attention it was not then receiving. I focused on the earlier work because I believed it to be both in style and content much more daring than the work she produced later. Since I was choosing to pursue both an academic career and the path of becoming a writer, there was a twofold purpose in my concentrated study of Morrison's work. She had become for me via her work a literary mentor—a guiding light. Had *The Bluest Eye* never been published it would have taken much more effort for me to write a memoir of black girlhood more than twenty years later. Speaking about the concerns that led her to write her first book Morrison commented: "I wrote about a victim who is a child and adults don't write about children. . . . I did not think it would be widely distributed because it was about things that probably nobody was interested in except me. I was reading a kind of book I had never read before." When *The Bluest Eye* was first published in 1970 I was a senior in high school. I was among the first generation in our family to attend college. Raised in a working-class family where the mouths to feed and the needs to be met were much greater than the income my daddy brought home from his hard work as a janitor at the post office, I knew firsthand what it was like to long for material objects that could never be possessed.

Reading Morrison's novel I felt the reality I had come from was recognized. It was not the sexual exploitation of the little girl Pecola that captured my attention. I could not identify with this experience. In the cosseted world of my southern black extended family girls were protected. It was Claudia's longings that captured me. Her desire to know the how and why of everything. It was her desire to confront and leave behind the shame of not having enough money that resonated with my girlhood experience. A continuum of longing to read books about little black girls exists between Morrison's reasons for writing this book and my reasons for reading it. In the introduction to my girlhood memoirs, I pay tribute to

Morrison for charting this journey, for daring to place little working-class black girls and their welfare at the center of the literary landscape.

In the more than twenty years since the publication of *The Bluest Eye* the trajectory of writing about girlhood has expanded. During that time, Morrison's literary career blossomed, culminating in her receiving a Nobel Prize for literature. Her acceptance of this honor was an incredible triumph in that it let the world know that great writing emerges from diverse locations, that it is not the province of any one race or gender. Hopefully, such recognition means that it will never be possible to push writing by black women into the shadows, dismissing it as lacking in merit or value. Historically, black women writers have had to write in a cultural climate where racism and sexism had already put in place a set of assumptions about the nature of "great" writing that automatically excluded black females. Historically racist/sexist stereotypes about the nature of black womanhood meant that the literary establishment was convinced that black women writers were incapable of creating serious imaginative writing.

As a consequence every black woman who takes pen in hand must be a resisting writer—one who does not let these assumptions inform her work. She must continue to believe she is as capable of becoming a great writer as those who have always been deemed capable of greatness, the largely white and male members of the American literary canon. All too often aspiring young black female writers abandon a concern with serious writing because they believe their work will not receive a fair hearing or just rewards. It astonished many readers that individuals within the mainstream literary establishment, which had for some time praised Morrison's work, were more than ready to express doubts about its value after she was awarded the Nobel Prize. It is a testimony to the strength of sexist/racist assumptions about "greatness" that the excellence of Morrison's writing would be called into question only as it was being recognized globally as having lasting merit and value. Her literary achievement was an outright challenge to old assumptions.

That her presence in the company of Nobel laureates threatened institutionalized structures of racism and sexism became most evident as individuals attempted to undermine her moment of glory by seeking to discredit her work. Significantly, individual black male writers were among those who sought to diminish its value. Writers who had never before felt the need to critically evaluate the merits of any chosen Nobel laureate suddenly felt called to "discredit" Morrison, revealing how deep the need is to reinscribe old structures of domination when those structures are being fundamentally challenged.

Beyond her writing, which is her marvelous gift to world culture, Morrison clearly realized the radical political significance of her receiving this honor—that the recognition of her value as a writer intervenes on racist and sexist assumptions about whose work can and should be seen as valuable. She knows that she has broken new ground. In her acceptance speech she spoke of eagerly anticipating the work of writers to come: "Those who, even as I speak, are mining, sifting, and polishing languages for illuminations none of us has dreamed of. But whether or not any one of them secures a place in this pantheon, the gathering of these writers is unmistakable and mounting." Significantly, by evoking the presence of gifted, though not yet heralded, writers, Morrison skillfully deconstructed any attempt to represent her work as an anomaly.

A popular magazine asked me to write a short piece about the impact of Morrison's Nobel Prize, particularly its impact on black women writers. They wanted confirmation of their assumption that the increased interest in popular writing by black women, pulp fiction and the like, was a direct result of her success. My response did not interest them. I pointed to the historical fact that lone individual black women writers had always written popular books that were incredibly successful. Throughout our literary history this work has garnered both audience attention and monetary reward. The momentum that black woman writers of popular fiction, like Terry McMillan, thrive on is quite different from the cultural currents that determine the reception of writers who are concerned more with craft and literary excellence than mass appeal. Without in any way diminishing the value of popular literature both black women readers and the entire reading public need to acknowledge the diversity of black women's writing. We can enjoy and appreciate the success of popular writing and the pleasure this work brings without taking it too seriously.

No doubt the reading public, which could appreciate Morrison's depth and complexity when reading her novels yet sought to diminish her work in the wake of the Nobel Prize, is far more comfortable imagining that a continuum exists between this work (i.e., popular fiction by black females) and her work rather than that of other Nobel laureates. Sadly, Morrison's success did not lead publishers to encourage and search for aspiring young black women writing serious fiction. There are still way too many editors in publishing who never read works by black women. And mass media is much more interested in limiting the scope of black female literary imaginations to the writing of popular fiction. The success of the already bourgeoning market in popular fiction by black women was often used to deflect attention away from the cultural significance of Morrison's triumph. Graciously and wisely she repudiated accolades that would represent her as an anomaly, as an exception to accepted racist and sexist stereotypes that imply that women, and especially black women, cannot do great writing. Still, embedded in the publishing world's tacit refusal to seize the moment and encourage aspiring young women writers, especially black females, to seek publication of their work is the assumption that this writing simply does not exist. This assumption subtly implies that Morrison is the grand exception. Usually those few contemporary black women writers whose work is deemed "serious" by the literary establishment are immigrant writers, mostly of Caribbean descent. Despite the success of diverse fiction by Jamaica Kincaid, she is not seen by critics as pandering to a taste in popular literature, nor does anyone question her capacity to do serious work. Nor does anyone question the writing skills of younger immigrant women writers following in her wake. And there is no reason why they should. Many of these young writers cite Toni Morrison's work as a literary influence. It is more than unfortunate that no such critical respect is given the aspiring indigenous black female writer.

While serious writing by aspiring young black females is mostly ignored or poorly underpublished by the publishing world, sensational popular works that are rarely skillfully crafted are projected as personifying the scope and trajectory of black women's writing. Such thinking feeds racist and sexist biases and simultaneously dissuades aspiring writers from focusing on serious writing. Writing imaginative work that is visionary and well crafted takes discipline and time. The aspiring black female writer who is encouraged by the possibility of huge advances to put forth work that is sensational, incomplete, or poorly crafted is done a disservice by the publishing industry. When such work receives instant attention and reward, the incentive to work at developing skill and craft is removed.

While it is evident that Morrison's literary achievements have opened a previously closed door, aspiring writers must rise to the challenge. Any black female who chooses to devote herself to craft, to serious writing, is far more likely to gain a wider public hearing now that the world has made known its longing to hear such voices via its celebration of Morrison's artistry. The success of her writing has intensified that longing. However, racist and sexist assumptions about who is capable of "good" or "great" work will rule the day until a body of serious writing by diverse black women appears. Those individuals who refuse to let these assumptions go will remain as dismissive of Morrison's work as they are of work by any writer from a marginal group. These narrow-minded readers will always be more eager to praise popular writing by black women, which they see as necessarily substandard (i.e., who can fault a group for not creating serious fictions when they are already deemed incapable of performing well on this terrain). They turn their backs on black female literary genius. Or if they do not completely devalue serious writing by black females, they try to convince the reading public that such writers are merely exceptions.

When I was a young writer striving to create serious work, I learned the importance of craft by reading and studying the work of gifted writers from all walks of life. Morrison's work was not the only guiding light, but it was one of the most valuable. Her fiction, interviews, essays all taught me to take the craft of writing seriously, to understand that it requires discipline and hard work. My admiration of her work has led me to be a rigorous reader, critical yet always respectful. Teaching her work in literature courses I watch the way the lyrical intensity of her words grips the reader, compelling them to ponder both the text they are reading and the creative process that made the writing possible. Early on in her first novel Morrison reminds readers that imagination without skill is not enough, that critical fictions must be carefully orchestrated. While we do not need work that is a poor imitation of her writing, we do need to let that writing inspire us to create artful fictions.

Toni Morrison's work is uniquely her own. She is an exceptional writer by any standard. She is not the only gifted black woman writer. Knowing this, she has adamantly resisted tokenization that is demeaning and patronizing. In the closing remarks of her Nobel Prize acceptance speech she informed the world, "It is, therefore, mindful of the gifts of my predecessors, the blessing of my sisters, in joyful anticipation of writers to come that I accept the honor the Swedish Academy has done me, and ask you to share what is for me a moment of grace." That grace embraces the historical legacy of black women writers, the writing that is being done now, and the writing to come. Like all acts of grace, it is everlasting.

writer to writer

remembering toni cade bambara

Toni Cade Bambara edited the anthology *The Black Woman* in 1970. It was groundbreaking. Together, a body of black women writers, critical thinkers, and/or activists were discussing the intersection of race and gender. Articles critically interrogated the sexism within black liberation struggle. Black women spoke about the pain and power of parenting, about poverty, about the devaluation of black womanhood. I was a senior in high school when this anthology was first published. Commenting on her decision to edit this work in an interview with Louis Massiah, Bambara acknowledged that she wanted to do a groundbreaking book that would refute the common assumption that black women were not engaged with thinking about gender roles or challenging sexism. Remembering the difficulty of finding a publisher she shared: "We began running around to the publishing houses and I began running into a lot of people I used to go to school with, white folks. They are saying things like, 'I've seen fabulous manuscripts from Black women, but they wind up on the sludge pile because there is no market for

Black women's works.' So then I got this idea: Never mind the papers from the Panther party women; let me do a book that will kick the door open. . . . My attention at that time was on kicking the door open so that other Black women's manuscripts could get a hearing and they certainly did." Singlehandedly, the anthology *The Black Woman* placed black women at the center of various feminist debates. It legitimized looking at black life from a feminist perspective.

It was groundbreaking because Toni Cade Bambara's powerful essay "On the Issue of Roles" broke traditional taboos precluding public discussions of gender conflict between black women and men. This piece was one of the first essays on feminist theory that looked at the interlocking relations between race, sex, and class. Bambara's perspective was revolutionary for its time. Had she become a major spokesperson for black liberation struggle, had her insistence that black men critique their sexism been taken seriously, the more militant dimensions of black freedom struggle would have transformed the lives of black people everywhere. This essay did transform the lives of individual black women readers. It inspired me to explore more deeply the impact of sexism on black life. Even though everyone active in feminist movement was reading this anthology when it was first published (it was so rare to have the diverse voices of black womanhood represented), mainstream white feminist thinkers were not eager to promote Bambara because the revolutionary feminism she espoused included a critique of racism and capitalism. Her perspective, which included resistance to imperialism, threatened reformist feminist focus on attaining gender equality within the existing social structure. Toni Cade Bambara wanted to challenge and transform the existing structure.

The publication of this anthology not only helped compel the publishing industry to recognize that there was a market for books by and about black women, it helped to create an intellectual climate where feminist theory focusing on black experience could emerge. Without the publication of this anthology, later feminist works focusing on black life might never have been written. The existence of this anthology certainly was a catalyst for my early feminist work. It was a beacon light. Whenever I became discouraged that there would be no audience for the feminist theory I was writing, I simply recalled the worn and tattered copies of this anthology that were passed around. It was a reminder that there was an audience eager to hear news about our lives.

Like Lorraine Hansberry, Bambara became a literary mentor for me because she was a critical thinker who wrote across many genres. I wanted to write work that would cross many barriers and speak to diverse communities even as I wanted to stay rooted in the southern black folk traditions that had sparked my creativity, my desire to write. Throughout her life Bambara was a champion of the black poor and working class. Since I first read her work as a young student coming from a southern working-class background, it was affirming that our vernacular traditions were beautifully evoked in her stories. Few black writers have captured the wit and humor of black life as skillfully as Bambara. She recognized the role of laughter in struggles for decolonization. To her, laughter was a way to dissent. The oppositional perspectives black people used to resist dehumanization were consistently evoked in her stories.

I first met Bambara when she was living in Atlanta, Georgia. We met at a conference focusing on black women and feminism at Spelman College. Feminist scholar and director of the women's center Beverly Guy-Sheftall introduced us. In those days I was shy in crowds and liked to be in the background when I felt uncomfortable. However, it was impossible to feel uncomfortable around

Toni. She was this incredible embodiment of African and southern hospitality. She knew how to make one feel welcome. She put me at ease. Coming from a working-class southern background I often felt I lacked necessary protocol, the bourgeois demeanor valued in certain settings. Bambara affirmed that it was better to forget decorum and "just be real." Most working-class black people who encountered Toni fondly remember her warmth and welcoming nature. As I heard one woman say: "She don't put on airs and try to make you think you don't know nothing." From the moment we met Bambara praised my writing and encouraged me to write more.

During my undergraduate years I met many writers who did not all live the spirit of their work, who were threatened when in the presence of aspiring young writers. By the time I met Toni I was sorely disillusioned. I understood by then that the work of a writer's imagination might indicate very little about her or his beliefs, her or his habits of being. I had met too many black writers who wrote didactically about the need to embrace "the people" who were deeply hierarchical, who liked lording it over others. The hypocrisy of the black middle class revolted me. Most writing about black life was done by privileged individuals who created poor and inadequate representations of the black masses. We were their subjects but they seemed to know nothing about our lives.

Toni Bambara was different. She loved blackness. She loved black people. She did not stand at a distance and write about the black masses. She lived among poor black people, in the segregated world of the South. Her love of regular everyday black folks was not sentimental. She was not a tourist. Her love was nurtured and sustained by keen political insights, an understanding of the importance of decolonization. It was she who most championed decolonization as an intimate process, telling us that "revolution begins in the self and with the self." While her love of black folks, and poor

233

black folks in particular, was a natural thing she understood its political implications in white supremacist capitalist patriarchy. Spreading that love, displaying it, offering it to all and sundry who came her way was a powerful dimension of her political activism. Everyday life was the site for transformation and change.

Late one night I went with Beverly to Toni's house in Atlanta. We had called to warn her we were on our way and planning to stay awhile. She let us know that her cupboards were bare 'cause she had been too busy working to get the domestic thing together and that her place was untidy as usual, but that we would be welcomed. We were. When we entered the cluttered world of Toni she urged us to just push stuff out of the way and make ourselves comfortable. She offered us unconditional acceptance and we gave that to her in return. Who could care about housekeeping when we had precious little time to converse with one another? Days and nights spent in her company engaged in fierce intellectual dialectical debate and dialogue were inspiring. An avid reader of periodicals and books, Toni's down-home manner often deflected attention away from the scope of her intellectual insights. I had never met a black woman writer as generous with her time and ideas as Toni Cade Bambara. She was always willing to nurture young writers and thinkers. She embodied for me the kind of writer I wanted to be—always in solidarity with my people, always struggling for justice for everyone, and always willing to sacrifice.

Everybody close to Toni knows that she could have had a different life, not a life where she was constantly struggling to make ends meet. She could have been part of the literary mainstream but that was not her nature. Her nature was bohemian; she liked to live life on the edge. And like all bohemians she was often critiqued by those around her who were frustrated that she was not living the life of the "great writer" that was the stuff of their imaginations. She invented the life that she wanted to live. And she lived this life on her own terms. This is the aspect of Bambara that more conservative folks found both incomprehensible and reprehensible. To them she was "mad" not to take the good jobs she could have taken in predominately white colleges in all-white communities. She was the high priestess of community, understanding the extent to which black survival is dependent on our capacity to make and live in community. She chose her communities. Often the manner in which she chose was reckless and haphazard but that is the nature of real community. It is a place where we learn to live comfortably with imperfections and contradictions.

In this way I could never be like Toni even though she was a mentor for me. I love solitude and order, everything in its place and a place for everything. She respected my choices and I respected hers. When she came to my minimalist flat she marveled at my capacity to live with so little, signifying and joking about the way I lived. Toni appreciated me for being me. Many times she would tease me about the way my mind works, telling me: "Girl, I just love to watch you thinking." No idea shared with Toni, no theory was too far-fetched to be considered. This unswerving support from a fellow writer was deeply affirming. As a critical thinker she treasured open-mindedness. While I often threatened others with my clarity of speech, my insights, Toni always told me that these were my gifts.

I was not in regular close contact with Toni. We did not hang together on a consistent basis. Our natures were too different to make for sustained intimacy. We were in the deepest sense of the word comrades in struggle, two black women who realized in our encounters with each other the power and pleasure of feminist sisterhood. We communicated about work and ideas. We played together. We respected each other. When other folks rebuked and scorned me, Toni would respond by writing the encouraging letter—making the don't-let-it-get-you-down phone call. She supported dissenting voices. I dedicated *Sisters of the Yam: Black Women and Self-Recovery* to Toni because it was the literary magic of her novel *The Salt Eaters* that cast a spell on me and made me think more deeply about issues of depression and isolation in black female life.

We talked about this dedication. Toni shared that she did not want anyone to think she was not still on the journey towards self-recovery because she was. That did not matter. It mattered that she had raised in this novel a clarion call for black females to stir from our psychic slumbers, to rise and rescue ourselves and one another. In her introduction to a collection of Bambara's work published posthumously, her dear friend and comrade Toni Morrison writes: "I don't know if she knew the heart cling of her fiction. Its pedagogy, its use, she knew very well, but I have often wondered if she knew how brilliant at it she was. There was no division in her mind between optimism and ruthless vigilance; between aesthetic obligation and the aesthetics of obligation." Like many of her readers who were her peers, Morrison fully appreciates Bambara's imaginative powers, her capacity to use black vernacular in a manner intensely poetic, lyrical, and accessible.

There are those individuals who are disappointed with Toni. They wanted her to write more, be more practical, live life on the terms that they would have chosen—terms that might have provided safety and stability. They resent her for the messes she made that they elected to try and tidy (those of us who knew girlfriend know that she never expected anyone to do anything that they did not willingly choose to do). She was not a creature of obligations. She did not expect a return on the care she gave. She gave freely and expected others to do the same.

When Toni was critically ill and it was evident that she would soon die, mutual women friends called to say I should contact her. I did not want to call Toni for fear I might be intruding. I did not want to impose an unnatural intimacy on us. I called though. We had several conversations. In all of them she was vibrant. I could feel the full force of her reckless and generous nature and it delighted me. She was dying as she had lived. And she was still welcoming me. Our last conversation was not about death or writing; Toni wanted to talk seriously with me about her concern that I was working too much. She felt I was allowing myself to become too isolated, that I needed to get out more, to socialize—to have more fun. We talked about the fun times we had shared. We talked about the place of pleasure in our lives. She wanted me to remember that pleasure is political—for the capacity to relax and play renews the spirit and makes it possible for us to come to the work of writing clearer, ready for the journey.

Those who attended to Toni in her last days and throughout the period of her illness may be convinced that she was not ready for her journey because she was unprepared in more ways than one. What they may fail to see is that she had already embraced this final journey when she chose to sacrifice a life of material comfort and acclaim to take the hard road. She was ready. She had been preparing herself her whole life to go the hard way. And to be at peace with that, with contradictions, with protracted struggle, with fate. I was blessed to be given an opportunity to share that peace with her in our last conversations. She taught me much about how to live as a black woman writer in this world. Even in the midst of her dying she was teaching me still.